Fluency Fundamentals

(The Prosody/Fluency Slice of the Full Circle)

By Randi Whitney

Fluency Fundamentals: Empowering Teachers to Build Confident, Expressive Readers

ISBN: 978-1-966301-28-8

Published by BIG Time Publishing Company

For permissions or inquiries, contact:

BIG Time Publishing Company
3502 Columbia Memorial Parkway, Kemah, TX 77565, 281-549-4466
randiwhitney.com

This book is a work of non-fiction. Any references to real events, people, or organizations are intended only to provide context and support the author's perspective and are used with permission when applicable.

All photos and drawings are original and belong to Randi Whitney.

First Edition: 2025
Printed in the United States of America

Randi Whitney's Library Card!

Enjoy all the books across multiple genres by Randi Whitney

Children's Books

Buffalo Nickel Ranch
Who Let the Goat Out
I Love Buggy Rides
The Messes We Make
The Annual Cookie Tree
It's Valentines, of Course of Course
The Community Can
Be Three
Leaving Tracks
The Blue Egg
The Class with Heart
Leave Something Take Something
Tomato Boy
Every Letter Counts
Chocolate Chip Cookies
Louis, Louis

Young Children's Chapter Books

The Ranch Coin
Buggy Rides
The Great Goatsby
The Community Colection
The Cookie Tree Tradition
The Biggest Mess
The Green Egg
The Lost Medal

Early Reader Picture Books

The Other Side of the Nickel
The Goat's Gate

Educational Books

Reading for Retrieval
Writing for Purpose
Teach BIG: Believe in Greatness – Bring Best Practices Back
Teach BIG: Believe in Greatness – Study Guide
4 Dimensions of Comprehension
Grammatical Matters
Lexicon Mysteries Solved
Fluency Flows
GAP Phonics: Preventing and Closing Gaps

Mystery/Thriller Novels

A Good Witness
The Knock
The Teacher Retreat
Twisted Poison

Christian Novels

The Last Day
The First Day

Motivational Books

Don't Spend Your CAN Years CAN'Ting

Preteen Christian Chapter Books

The Bookcase: Matthew
The Bookcase: Mark
The Bookcase: Luke
The Bookcase: John
The Bookcase: Acts
The Bookcase: Romans

randiwhitney.com
teachbig.com

Philosophy for Teaching Reading Fluency

Fluency is not just the ability to read words accurately and quickly; it is the seamless connection between decoding, comprehension, expression, and the rhythm of language. Fluency serves as the bridge between learning to read and reading to learn. My philosophy for teaching fluency is grounded in the belief that fluency is developed through intentional, systematic, and engaging practices that combine evidence-based strategies with opportunities for creative and meaningful reading experiences. Students become fluent readers when they are equipped with the tools to decode accurately, read with natural expression, and engage deeply with text.

The Cornerstones of Fluency Instruction

1. **Structured Foundations with Direct Decodables** Direct decodable texts are the cornerstone of fluency instruction. Students must first build accuracy through texts that align with their phonics knowledge. These texts ensure that 90% or more of the words can be decoded using previously taught skills, creating a pathway for success. By starting with direct decodables, students gain confidence in their ability to decode while practicing fluency with manageable and meaningful content.
2. **Repeated Reading for Mastery** Repeated reading is essential for building fluency. Through multiple readings of the same text, students transition from focusing on decoding to reading with accuracy, speed, and expression. This practice strengthens automaticity and allows students to internalize language patterns, improving their ability to read more complex texts over time. Repeated readings also foster confidence, as students experience measurable growth with each attempt.
3. **Choral Reading for Collective Confidence** Choral reading allows students to experience the rhythm and flow of language in a supportive, group setting. By reading aloud together, students learn pacing, intonation, and expression while benefiting from the collective voice of the group. Choral reading also builds a sense of community, encouraging hesitant readers to participate and learn through collaboration.
4. **Memorization: A Lost Art Revived** Memorization plays a pivotal role in fluency development. By committing texts like poems, speeches, or famous passages to memory, students internalize the natural cadence, inflection, and phrasing of language. Memorization not only enhances oral fluency but also strengthens silent reading comprehension by reinforcing rhythm and tone. The act of practicing and performing memorized texts builds confidence and provides a meaningful way to engage with language.
5. **Intonation and Expression: The Heart of Fluency** Intonation, stress, and expression transform reading from robotic to dynamic. Students must learn how vocal emphasis can change meaning and convey emotion. By practicing sentences with varied stress, such as "I didn't say she stole my pencil," students explore how tone influences interpretation. Teaching students to read with intentional expression ensures their fluency aligns with comprehension, making their reading engaging and purposeful.
6. **Drama: Bringing Text to Life** Drama provides a rich, interactive way to develop fluency. Scripts require students to read dialogue with expression, pacing, and attention to stage directions, such as "[whispering nervously]" or "[shouting excitedly]." Through

rehearsing and performing plays, students learn to convey tone, mood, and character while building their confidence in oral reading. Drama helps students connect with text on a deeper level, making reading both engaging and memorable.

7. **Poetry and Rhyme: The Music of Language** Poetry and rhyme are natural tools for fluency practice. Their inherent rhythm and repetition make them ideal for teaching pacing, phrasing, and intonation. Poems like "Twinkle, Twinkle, Little Star" or Robert Frost's "Stopping by Woods on a Snowy Evening" encourage students to experiment with rhythm and expression. Poetry also fosters creativity and a love for language, making fluency practice both enjoyable and meaningful.
8. **True Content: Fluency with Purpose** Fluency practice should be rooted in meaningful content that expands students' knowledge and curiosity. Whether reading about the life cycle of a frog, the Industrial Revolution, or the invention of the steam engine, students develop fluency while engaging with authentic, rich texts. Content-based fluency instruction not only improves reading skills but also deepens comprehension and builds background knowledge, connecting fluency to learning across disciplines.

Guiding Principles for Fluency Instruction

- **Fluency is a Journey:** Every student progresses at their own pace. Instruction must be tailored to meet students where they are while challenging them to grow.
- **Fluency Requires Repetition:** Mastery comes from practice. Students need repeated opportunities to read the same text in varied ways to build confidence and skill.
- **Fluency is Expressive:** Reading fluency goes beyond speed; it's about bringing text to life with tone, emotion, and comprehension.
- **Fluency is Collaborative:** Group activities like choral reading and drama provide supportive environments where students learn from one another.
- **Fluency Connects to Content:** Engaging with meaningful texts enhances fluency while expanding knowledge and curiosity.

The Goal of Fluency Instruction

The ultimate goal of fluency instruction is to create confident, engaged readers who approach texts with curiosity, comprehension, and joy. Fluent readers are better equipped to access the world of ideas, stories, and information that reading provides. Through direct decodables, repeated practice, expressive techniques, and meaningful content, students develop fluency not as a mechanical skill but as a dynamic and purposeful way of engaging with language.

By embracing these strategies, we empower students to read with confidence, clarity, and passion—skills that will serve them in the classroom and beyond. Fluency flows naturally when students are equipped with the tools to decode, express, and connect, making reading a lifelong source of learning and enjoyment.

Special note: **Each chapter will contain approximately three lesson plans to further enhance the concept of the chapter. Keep in mind, it is not expected for you to complete all of these lesson plans. They are provided to help you glean an overall schema or understanding for the chapter. You are invited to use the lesson plans but also enhance them with your own creativity or use the prescribed curriculum you have in place.**

Fluency Fundamentals Chapter Breakdown with Corresponding Resources

Chapter Number	Chapter Title	Accompanying Materials
1	**Model Fluent Reading**	*Fluency Flows, Prosody Practice for Science, Prosody Practice for Social Studies*
2	**Choral Reading**	*Full Circle Comprehension for Science, Full Circle Comprehension for Social Studies*
3	**Paired Reading**	*Power Graph Power*
4	**Rewind Reading**	*Teach Big Online Assessment Platform*
5	**Reader's Theater**	*Fluency Flows, Buffalo Nickel Ranch Dramas, Decodable Dramas, Holiday Dramas*
6	**Fluency Centers**	*Fluency Flows, Prosody Practice for Science, Prosody Practice for Social Studies*
7	**Audio-Assisted Reading**	*Teach Big Online Assessment Platform*
8	**Timed Readings**	*Teach Big Online Assessment Platform*
9	**Echo Reading (Repeat Reading)**	*Fluency Flows, Full Circle Composition for Science, Full Circle Composition for Social Studies*
10	**Flashcard Fluency**	*High-Frequency Word Family Booklets, I Spy Fry Phrases, Word Family Booklets*
11	**Sentence Scrambles**	*Elaboration Station*
12	**Direct Decodable Text Reading**	*Direct Decodables, Decodable Dramas*
13	**Close Reading Exercises**	*Fluency Flows*
14	**Oral Book Summaries**	*No Product at this Time*
15	**Poetry Practice**	*Extension Project for Children's Book Tomato Boy, Extension Book for I Love Buggy Rides*
16	**Small-Group Interventions**	*Extension Project for Children's Book Tomato Boy, Extension Book for I Love Buggy Rides*

17	**Self-Monitoring Strategies**	*Direct Decodables, Paragraph Power, Selection Collection*
18	**Technology Integration**	*Teach Big Online Assessment Platform*
19	**Fluency Graphing**	*Fluency Flows*
20	**Daily Independent Reading**	*Selection Collections*
21	**Dramas and Fluency: Bringing Reading to Life**	*Decodable Dramas, Holiday Dramas, Buffalo Nickel Ranch Dramas, Fluency Flows*
22	**Memorization: The Missing Link to Fluency Today**	*Full Circle Comprehension, Fluency Flows*
23	**What Exactly Did You Say? Changing Emphasis**	*Prosody Practice*

Chapter Outline for Fluency Instruction Strategies

1. **Model Fluent Reading**
   - **Explanation:** Demonstrate appropriate pace, expression, and intonation while reading aloud.
   - **Example:** Read *The Three Little Pigs* using varied tones for characters to engage students.
2. **Choral Reading**
   - **Explanation:** The class reads aloud in unison to practice fluency together.
   - **Example:** Use the poem *Jack and Jill*, focusing on rhythm and pacing.
3. **Paired Reading**
   - **Explanation:** Pair fluent readers with less fluent peers to model fluency and build confidence.
   - **Example:** Partners take turns reading a passage, mimicking each other's pacing and tone.
4. **Rewind Reading**
   - **Explanation:** Students read the same passage multiple times to improve fluency.
   - **Example:** Use a paragraph about a cat's adventures, timing the first and last attempts.
5. **Reader's Theater**
   - **Explanation:** Perform scripts aloud to encourage practice with expression and fluency.
   - **Example:** Assign roles from *Goldilocks and the Three Bears* and practice expressive delivery.
6. **Fluency Centers**
   - **Explanation:** Rotational stations with targeted fluency activities.
   - **Example:** Include whisper phones and one-minute timed reading stations.
7. **Audio-Assisted Reading**
   - **Explanation:** Students listen to recordings of fluent reading while following along in the text.
   - **Example:** Use *Green Eggs and Ham* with an audio recording for practice.
8. **Timed Readings**
   - **Explanation:** Students read a passage for one minute to focus on speed and accuracy.
   - **Example:** Use a passage about penguins, tracking correct words per minute.
9. **Echo Reading (Repeat Reading)**
   - **Explanation:** The teacher reads aloud, and students repeat it, mimicking the modeled fluency.
   - **Example:** "The dog barked loudly" read with expressive emphasis.
10. **Flashcard Fluency**
    - **Explanation:** Practice sight words or short phrases using flashcards.
    - **Example:** Use phrases like "the big brown bear" for quick recognition practice.

11. **Sentence Scrambles**
    - **Explanation:** Students reorder scrambled sentences to improve fluency and comprehension.
    - **Example:** Rearrange "went store the Sally to" into "Sally went to the store."
12. **Direct Decodable Text Reading**
    - **Explanation:** Provide texts matched to students' reading levels for targeted fluency practice.
    - **Example:** Use *Frog and Toad Are Friends* for second-grade readers.
13. **Close Reading Exercises**
    - **Explanation:** Provide passages with missing words for students to fill in while reading aloud.
    - **Example:** "The ___ jumped over the moon" with students supplying "cow."
14. **Oral Book Summaries**
    - **Explanation:** Students present summaries aloud, focusing on clarity and expression.
    - **Example:** Summarize *Charlotte's Web* with emphasis on key events.
15. **Poetry Practice**
    - **Explanation:** Use poetry's rhythm and rhyme for fluency practice.
    - **Example:** Practice *Twinkle, Twinkle, Little Star* multiple times for rhythm and pacing.
16. **Small-Group Interventions**
    - **Explanation:** Work intensively with small groups to address specific fluency challenges.
    - **Example:** Focus on decoding multisyllabic words like "elephant."
17. **Self-Monitoring Strategies**
    - **Explanation:** Teach students to recognize and correct reading errors.
    - **Example:** Guide a student to reread and self-correct "cap" to "cat."
18. **Technology Integration**
    - **Explanation:** Use apps for feedback and independent fluency practice.
    - **Example:** Use a reading app for students to record and review their readings.
19. **Fluency Graphing**
    - **Explanation:** Chart fluency progress visually to motivate improvement.
    - **Example:** Students plot their words-per-minute scores weekly.
20. **Daily Independent Reading**
    - **Explanation:** Consistent, student-selected silent reading to build fluency.
    - **Example:** Provide a variety of books like *Diary of a Wimpy Kid* for 15-minute sessions.
21. **Dramas and Fluency: Bringing Reading to Life**
    - **Explanation:** Use scripts and performances to develop fluency through expression and tone.
    - **Example:** Students perform *The Three Billy Goats Gruff*, focusing on dramatic delivery.

22. **Memorization: The Missing Link to Fluency Today**
    - **Explanation:** Teach students to memorize and recite short texts to reinforce rhythm, tone, and pacing.
    - **Example:** Memorize and recite Robert Frost's *Stopping by Woods on a Snowy Evening.*
23. **What Exactly Did You Say? Changing Emphasis on One Word Changes the Meaning**
    - **Explanation:** Show how emphasizing different words in a sentence can change its meaning.
    - **Example:** Use "I didn't say he stole the money" and shift emphasis to different words to explore how it alters the intent.

This expanded outline provides a comprehensive roadmap for incorporating fluency-building strategies across various contexts and instructional styles.

Reading Fluency Background

Interesting Info about Reading Fluency

Here are some intriguing and lesser-known facts about acquiring reading fluency that teachers might find valuable:

1. Fluency is Closely Linked to Listening Skills

- Fluent readers often have strong auditory processing skills. Listening to fluent reading, such as through read-alouds or audio-assisted reading, helps students internalize the rhythm, tone, and pacing of language. This is particularly beneficial for struggling readers.

2. Silent Reading Fluency is Different from Oral Fluency

- Silent reading fluency develops later than oral fluency because it relies on internalized prosody (reading with expression in your mind). Students may read fluently aloud but struggle with comprehension during silent reading until this skill is developed.

3. Chunking Text Affects Fluency

- Fluent readers group words into meaningful phrases or "chunks" rather than reading word-by-word. Teaching students how to chunk text can significantly improve their pacing, phrasing, and comprehension.

4. Repetition is Key—but Only with Purpose

- While repeated reading improves fluency, the impact is greatest when students understand *why* they are rereading (e.g., to improve expression, accuracy, or comprehension). Purposeful repetition prevents boredom and fosters deeper engagement with the text.

5. Memorization Supports Automaticity

- Memorizing meaningful texts (e.g., poems or speeches) helps students internalize language structures and vocabulary, which they can apply to new texts. This builds both fluency and long-term reading stamina.

6. Prosody Predicts Comprehension

- Students who read with natural expression and rhythm tend to have better comprehension. This is because prosody reflects understanding of the text's structure and meaning. Teachers can focus on prosody to identify students struggling with deeper comprehension.

7. Fluency and Vocabulary are Interconnected

- A robust vocabulary enhances fluency because students can quickly recognize and decode familiar words. Conversely, struggling readers often need explicit vocabulary instruction to improve their fluency.

8. Decodable Texts Aren't Just for Beginners

- Even intermediate readers can benefit from decodable texts when practicing specific phonics patterns or refining decoding skills. These texts build confidence and reinforce automaticity at all stages of reading development.

9. Fluency Training Can Improve Writing

- As students read fluently, they internalize grammatical structures, vocabulary, and sentence rhythms that transfer to their writing. Encouraging fluency practice can lead to more sophisticated written expression.

10. Physical Movement Enhances Fluency

- Multisensory activities, such as choral reading with actions or clapping to rhythm, activate multiple parts of the brain, reinforcing fluency skills. Movement engages kinesthetic learners and improves retention.

11. Timed Reading Isn't Just About Speed

- While words-per-minute (WPM) is a common fluency measure, the goal is not simply faster reading but more accurate and expressive reading. Teachers should emphasize balanced fluency, integrating speed with comprehension and prosody.

12. Fluency Plateaus Are Normal

- Many students experience a "fluency plateau" as they transition from decoding to reading for comprehension. During this time, their progress in WPM may slow, but they are often developing more nuanced skills like silent reading fluency or complex comprehension.

13. Stress and Anxiety Impact Fluency

- Students who feel nervous or pressured to perform often read less fluently. Creating a supportive and low-stress environment, such as using peer or small-group reading activities, helps students build confidence and improve their fluency.

14. Fluency Development Continues Into Adulthood

- Even adults refine their fluency as they encounter more complex texts and reading purposes. For students, fluency doesn't stop developing after elementary school; it evolves as texts increase in complexity and expectations shift.

By incorporating these insights into their teaching practices, educators can better support students on their journey to becoming fluent, confident readers.

Challenges to Teaching Reading Fluency

Teaching fluency can be challenging for many educators, as it requires balancing multiple elements of reading development while addressing diverse student needs. Here are some common challenges teachers face when teaching fluency:

---

1. Lack of Time for Targeted Practice

- **Challenge:** Teachers often struggle to find sufficient time in the day for fluency practice amid packed curricula and the demands of other subjects.
- **Impact:** Without consistent, focused practice, students may not develop the automaticity and expression necessary for fluent reading.

---

2. Differentiating Instruction

- **Challenge:** Students in the same classroom often have vastly different fluency levels, making it difficult to provide individualized instruction.
- **Impact:** Struggling readers may not receive enough support, while advanced readers may not be challenged appropriately.

---

3. Overemphasis on Speed

- **Challenge:** Many fluency assessments prioritize words-per-minute (WPM) as the primary metric, leading to an overemphasis on reading speed rather than comprehension or prosody.
- **Impact:** Students may focus on reading quickly rather than understanding the text, resulting in shallow reading habits.

---

4. Lack of Engagement

- **Challenge:** Students may find fluency practice repetitive or boring, especially when it involves repeated reading of the same text.
- **Impact:** Disengaged students are less likely to put effort into improving their fluency, hindering their progress.

---

5. Difficulty with Prosody

- **Challenge:** Teaching students to read with appropriate tone, pitch, and expression can be abstract and difficult to model effectively.
- **Impact:** Students may struggle to connect prosody with comprehension, leading to flat, monotone reading.

---

6. Managing Anxiety in Struggling Readers

- **Challenge:** Struggling readers often feel self-conscious or anxious about reading aloud, particularly in front of peers.
- **Impact:** Anxiety can lead to avoidance behaviors, less participation, and slower progress in developing fluency.

---

7. Insufficient Resources

- **Challenge:** Some classrooms lack a variety of high-quality, leveled texts or engaging materials for fluency practice, such as decodable books or scripts.
- **Impact:** Limited resources make it harder for teachers to tailor fluency practice to individual student needs.

---

8. Balancing Fluency with Comprehension

- **Challenge:** Teachers may find it difficult to ensure that fluency practice also supports comprehension rather than focusing solely on accuracy and speed.
- **Impact:** Students may become fluent decoders without truly understanding the text, resulting in a disconnect between fluency and overall reading ability.

---

9. Transitioning Silent Reading Fluency

- **Challenge:** While oral fluency is often emphasized, transitioning students to fluent silent reading is less structured and harder to monitor.
- **Impact:** Some students may struggle with comprehension and prosody in silent reading, even if their oral fluency is strong.

---

10. Addressing ELL and Diverse Needs

- **Challenge:** English Language Learners (ELLs) and students with learning differences may require additional supports for decoding, vocabulary, and prosody.
- **Impact:** Without targeted interventions, these students may fall behind in fluency development compared to their peers.

---

11. Limited Parental Involvement

- **Challenge:** Fluency practice often benefits from reinforcement at home, but not all parents are equipped or available to support reading practice.
- **Impact:** Inconsistent practice outside of school can slow student progress.

---

12. Monitoring and Tracking Progress

- **Challenge:** Measuring fluency in a meaningful and actionable way requires regular assessments, which can be time-consuming.
- **Impact:** Teachers may struggle to collect enough data to adjust instruction effectively for individual students.

---

13. Misconceptions About Fluency

- **Challenge:** Some educators or parents may view fluency as purely about speed rather than a combination of accuracy, expression, and comprehension.
- **Impact:** Misaligned expectations can lead to a narrow approach to fluency instruction, neglecting key components like prosody.

---

14. Addressing the Fluency Plateau

- **Challenge:** Many students hit a fluency plateau where their progress slows, often during the transition from early to intermediate reading skills.
- **Impact:** Without targeted support, these students may lose motivation and struggle to reach advanced fluency levels.

15. Integrating Technology Effectively

- **Challenge:** While digital tools can enhance fluency practice, not all teachers are familiar with how to integrate them meaningfully into their instruction.
- **Impact:** Technology may be underutilized or fail to meet its potential as a resource for fluency development.

By identifying and addressing these challenges, teachers can better support their students' journey toward becoming fluent, confident readers.

Common Myths About Teaching Reading Fluency to Children

1. **Myth: Fluency Is Just About Reading Fast**
    - **Reality:** While rate is a component of fluency, it also includes **accuracy** (reading words correctly) and **prosody** (reading with expression). Reading too quickly can compromise comprehension and lead to errors.
    - **Example:** A child who speeds through a passage without understanding the meaning is not truly fluent.

---

2. **Myth: Fluent Readers Don't Need to Practice Fluency**
    - **Reality:** Even students who appear fluent can benefit from ongoing fluency practice to improve expression, comprehension, and confidence. Reading aloud challenging texts helps them refine their skills further.
    - **Example:** Advanced readers may struggle with prosody when encountering texts with complex sentence structures or unfamiliar vocabulary.

---

3. **Myth: Silent Reading Automatically Builds Fluency**
    - **Reality:** Silent reading is beneficial for comprehension and vocabulary, but it doesn't inherently improve oral fluency. **Guided oral reading** with feedback is essential for developing pacing, accuracy, and expression.
    - **Example:** A student who silently reads well may stumble when reading aloud due to a lack of practice in oral fluency.

---

4. **Myth: Fluency Develops Naturally Without Instruction**
    - **Reality:** Fluency requires **explicit teaching** and structured practice. Simply exposing children to texts is not enough; they need strategies and feedback to improve.
    - **Example:** A struggling reader may need modeling, echo reading, or choral reading activities to learn proper intonation and phrasing.

5. **Myth: Memorizing Sight Words Is Enough for Fluency**
   - **Reality:** While sight word recognition is helpful, fluency also depends on **decoding skills**, comprehension, and the ability to read varied texts. Over-reliance on memorization can hinder students' ability to tackle unfamiliar words.
   - **Example:** A child who knows sight words might struggle with a text containing multisyllabic or less common vocabulary.

---

6. **Myth: Fluency Instruction Is Only for Younger Readers**
   - **Reality:** Fluency is a foundational skill but remains important throughout a student's education. Older readers may need fluency instruction for more complex texts, such as those with academic or technical language.
   - **Example:** High school students may struggle with fluency when reading historical documents or scientific passages aloud without prior practice.

---

7. **Myth: Fluency Practice Is Boring and Repetitive**
   - **Reality:** Fluency activities can be engaging when creative strategies are used, such as **reader's theater**, **poetry reading**, or **technology-based tools**. Students are more motivated when they enjoy the process.
   - **Example:** Performing a short play allows students to practice fluency in an interactive and fun way, making the repetition feel purposeful.

---

8. **Myth: Fluency and Comprehension Are Separate Skills**
   - **Reality:** Fluency and comprehension are deeply intertwined. Fluent readers use their skills to focus on understanding the text, while struggling fluency often hinders comprehension.
   - **Example:** A child who reads with poor fluency may not grasp the meaning of a text because they're focusing too much on decoding individual words.

---

9. **Myth: One-Size-Fits-All Approaches Work for Fluency**
   - **Reality:** Every child learns differently, and effective fluency instruction must be tailored to meet diverse needs. Struggling readers, advanced readers, and English Language Learners (ELLs) require different strategies.
   - **Example:** Struggling readers might benefit from phonics-focused fluency drills, while advanced readers may need expression-focused activities with complex texts.

10. **Myth: Technology Can Replace Teacher Guidance**
    - **Reality:** Technology is a valuable tool for fluency practice but cannot replace the feedback and individualized support that teachers provide. Tools work best when integrated into a broader instructional strategy.
    - **Example:** An app that provides immediate feedback on pronunciation complements, but doesn't substitute, teacher-led discussions about prosody and meaning.

---

11. **Myth: Fluency Is Only Relevant for Reading Aloud**
    - **Reality:** Fluency impacts both oral and silent reading. Fluent readers process text quickly and accurately, which boosts comprehension and enjoyment during silent reading.
    - **Example:** A fluent silent reader can summarize the main ideas of a text efficiently, while a less fluent reader may struggle to keep up with the content.

---

12. **Myth: Fluency Tests Are the Best Indicator of Progress**
    - **Reality:** While fluency assessments like words-per-minute (WPM) are helpful, they don't capture other aspects like comprehension, expression, or motivation. Progress should be measured holistically.
    - **Example:** A student might have a high WPM score but read monotone or fail to understand the text's meaning.

---

13. **Myth: Only Struggling Readers Need Modeling**
    - **Reality:** All students, regardless of reading ability, benefit from hearing fluent reading modeled regularly. It helps them understand tone, phrasing, and rhythm.
    - **Example:** Advanced readers may better appreciate the nuances of a Shakespearean play when the teacher models expressive reading.

---

14. **Myth: Fluency Should Be Perfect**
    - **Reality:** Fluency is a skill that develops over time, and minor mistakes are part of the process. The goal is improvement, not perfection.
    - **Example:** A student who self-corrects errors and continues reading smoothly is demonstrating fluency progress.

15. **Myth: Group Reading Always Builds Fluency**
    - **Reality:** While group reading can be helpful, without proper guidance, it may reinforce errors or discourage struggling readers. Structured activities like **choral reading** or **partner reading** are more effective.
    - **Example:** Assigning roles in a **reader's theater** activity ensures that students practice fluency collaboratively while focusing on individual strengths.

By addressing these myths, teachers can adopt more informed and effective strategies for fluency instruction, ensuring that all students thrive as readers.

Fluency TEKS

(4) Developing and sustaining foundational language skills: listening, speaking, reading, writing, and thinking - fluency. The student reads gray level text with fluency and comprehension. The student is expected to use appropriate fluency (rate, accuracy, and prosody) when reading grade level text.

Breakout Fluency TEKS

(i) use appropriate fluency (rate) when reading grade-level text
(ii) use appropriate fluency (accuracy) when reading grade-level text
(iii) use appropriate fluency (prosody) when reading grade-level text

RAP:

A Guide to Understanding and Mastering Fluency

Fluency is the bridge between decoding and comprehension, enabling readers to understand and enjoy text. To make fluency memorable for students and teachers, the acronym **RAP—Rate, Accuracy, and Prosody**—encapsulates its essential components. Each aspect of RAP contributes uniquely to a reader's ability to read smoothly, confidently, and with understanding.

RAP: Breaking Down the Elements

R - Rate

Definition: Reading at an appropriate speed to support comprehension without rushing or dragging.

- **Why it matters**: Reading too quickly can lead to skipped words and missed meaning, while reading too slowly can make it hard to maintain understanding and engagement.
- **Example**: A fluent reader adjusts their rate based on the text. They might read an exciting scene quickly, such as, "The car zoomed down the hill, tires screeching!" but slow down for a complex sentence in a science text: "The process of photosynthesis involves several intricate steps."

How to Practice:

- Use **timed readings** to help students find a comfortable reading pace.
- Practice **echo reading** where the teacher models appropriate pacing, and students mimic it.

A - Accuracy

Definition: Decoding and pronouncing words correctly.

- **Why it matters**: Misreading words disrupts meaning and comprehension. Accuracy ensures that students are interpreting the author's intended message.
- **Example**: A student reads the sentence, "The big brown dog barked loudly." If they misread "barked" as "baked," the sentence loses meaning and becomes confusing.

How to Practice:

- Use **decodable texts** aligned with phonics instruction to build strong decoding skills.
- Play **error-detection games**, where students listen to or read sentences and identify incorrect words.
- Focus on high-frequency words to reduce errors in common vocabulary.

P - Prosody

Definition: Reading with appropriate expression, tone, and phrasing to convey meaning and engage listeners.

- **Why it matters**: Prosody brings text to life, making it more engaging and easier to understand. It reflects the emotions, tone, and mood of the story.
- **Example**: Compare these two readings of a sentence:
    - Monotone: "Oh no the bridge is collapsing."
    - Expressive: "Oh no! The bridge is collapsing!" In the expressive version, changes in pitch and volume reflect the urgency and emotion of the situation.

How to Practice:

- Use **poetry and scripts** to practice reading with varied tones and rhythms.
- Discuss and model how **punctuation guides prosody** (e.g., pausing at commas, raising tone for questions).
- Encourage students to imagine they're **performing for an audience** to enhance expression.

Activities to Teach RAP

1. **Fluency RAP Charts**:
   - Create a chart with three columns: Rate, Accuracy, and Prosody. After reading a passage, students self-assess or peer-assess their performance in each category.
2. **Rate Relay**:
   - Provide three versions of a passage: slow, medium, and fast. Students practice reading each, then discuss which rate supports comprehension the best.
3. **Accuracy Spotlight**:
   - Highlight challenging words in a passage. Students practice decoding them first, then read the passage aloud to focus on accurate word recognition.
4. **Prosody Performances**:
   - Assign students a dialogue-heavy text, such as a play or a story with expressive characters. Have them practice reading with emotion and appropriate phrasing, then perform for the class.

The Importance of RAP in TEKS

Across grade levels, the **TEKS emphasize RAP** as essential for developing fluent readers. From decoding simple sentences in early grades to analyzing complex texts in middle and high school, RAP ensures students are prepared for the demands of academic and real-world reading. Teachers can use RAP as a daily framework to reinforce fluency skills, empowering students to become confident, expressive, and independent readers.

By mastering **Rate, Accuracy, and Prosody**, students don't just read—they bring stories and information to life!

Small Group Activities for RAP Fluency using Randi Whitney's Buffalo Nickel Ranch Children's Books Series

(all books available on amazon.com)

Book: I Love Buggy Rides

Activity 1: "Buggy Rhythm Echo"

- **Focus:** Prosody
- **Materials Needed:** Copies of a rhythmic passage from the book, tambourines, or clapping cues.
- **Instructions:**
    1. Select a rhythmic passage describing the buggy ride's pace (e.g., "Clip-clop, clip-clop, the buggy went up the hill").
    2. Model reading the passage with exaggerated rhythm and tone.
    3. Students echo the reading, mimicking the rhythm and prosody.
    4. Use tambourines or hand claps to help them keep pace and add emphasis to key words.

Assessment: Listen for correct pacing and expressive delivery. Provide feedback on intonation.
Intervention: Simplify the rhythm by breaking the sentence into smaller parts for repetition.
Enrichment: Have students act out the buggy's pace with body movements while reading.

Book: Tomato Boy

Activity 2: "Tomato Tone Detective"

- **Focus:** Accuracy and Prosody
- **Materials Needed:** Passages where Tomato Boy faces challenges, highlighter pens.
- **Instructions:**
    1. Select passages with emotional cues (e.g., "Tomato Boy wobbled on his vine. 'Will I ever be picked?' he wondered.").
    2. Discuss how emotions like doubt or hope affect tone.
    3. Have students highlight words or phrases that indicate emotions.
    4. Practice reading aloud, emphasizing tone shifts for phrases like "wobbled" or "wondered."

Assessment: Use a checklist to note tone changes and appropriate expression.
Intervention: Provide one-on-one modeling for students struggling with tone recognition.
Enrichment: Ask advanced students to rewrite a short scene, adding their stage directions for tone.

Book: <u>Who Let the Goat Out?</u>

Activity 3: "Fast and Accurate Goat Chase"

- **Focus:** Rate and Accuracy
- **Materials Needed:** Passages about the goat's escape, a timer, fluency tracking chart.
- **Instructions:**
    1. Choose an action-packed passage (e.g., "The goat dashed through the fence, knocking over buckets!").
    2. Model reading at different speeds, discussing how rate affects comprehension.
    3. Students practice reading the passage at a steady, clear pace.
    4. Time each student, noting their WPM (words per minute) and accuracy rate.

Assessment: Record WPM and note decoding errors. Celebrate improvements.
Intervention: Pair struggling readers with a partner for choral reading. Focus on short phrases.
Enrichment: Create a dramatic reading challenge where students add sound effects (e.g., stomping for the goat).

Summary

Each of these activities supports RAP fluency by engaging students with dynamic, story-specific tasks. They ensure that Rate, Accuracy, and Prosody are reinforced in a fun, memorable way tied to the themes and energy of your books.

Chapter 1

The Power of Modeling Fluent Reading

Fluent reading is the cornerstone of literacy. For young readers, seeing and hearing fluent reading modeled daily is one of the most effective ways to internalize the rhythm, pace, and expression of language. Teachers play a crucial role in this process by demonstrating fluent reading every day in their classrooms. This chapter will explore how modeling fluent reading engages students, develops their skills, and fosters a love of reading, while offering practical strategies and examples to bring this practice to life.

Why Model Fluent Reading?

Imagine a conductor guiding an orchestra. Without the conductor's expertise, the musicians might struggle to maintain rhythm, harmony, and balance. Similarly, a fluent reader demonstrates to students how language sounds when it flows seamlessly. It shows them how words are grouped into meaningful phrases, how punctuation guides expression, and how varied tones convey the writer's intent.

For elementary students, many of whom are just beginning to connect sounds to letters and letters to words, hearing a fluent reader helps them visualize how those sounds and words come together to create meaning. This practice also reinforces listening comprehension, a key skill that parallels reading comprehension.

Setting the Stage for Fluency

Modeling fluent reading doesn't require elaborate preparation. All it takes is an engaging text, a clear purpose, and an expressive delivery. Here are the key elements to keep in mind when reading aloud:

1. **Pace**
   The pace of reading should be steady—not too fast to confuse students, and not too slow to lose their attention. Students should hear how a natural pace allows the story or passage to unfold smoothly.

2. **Expression**
   Use your voice to bring characters and events to life. Vary your tone, pitch, and volume to match the mood of the text. For instance, whisper when a character is sneaking, or raise your voice during an exciting moment.
3. **Intonation**
   Intonation helps convey the meaning of sentences. For example, a question should sound inquisitive, while an exclamation should sound enthusiastic or alarmed.

Practical Strategies for Modeling Fluent Reading

1. **Choose Engaging Texts**
   Select books or passages that capture students' attention and encourage active listening. Books with dialogue, humor, or suspense, like *The Gruffalo* by Julia Donaldson or *Click, Clack, Moo: Cows That Type* by Doreen Cronin, are perfect for showcasing expression and intonation.
2. **Think Aloud as You Read**
   Pause occasionally to explain why you read a sentence in a particular way. For example, after reading, "The bear growled angrily," you might say, "Did you hear how my voice got low and gruff? That's because the text says the bear was angry."
3. **Emphasize Phrasing**
   Demonstrate how words are grouped together to create meaning. For example, read this sentence in two ways:
   - Incorrect: "The bear / growled / angrily."
   - Fluent: "The bear growled angrily."
     Explain how breaking words into natural phrases makes the sentence sound smoother and easier to understand.
4. **Invite Participation**
   After modeling, encourage students to echo your reading. Choose a line or paragraph and have them repeat it, mimicking your pace and tone. This active involvement reinforces what they've just heard.
5. **Use Predictable Texts**
   For younger students, predictable texts with repetition, rhyme, or rhythm help build confidence. Books like *Brown Bear, Brown Bear, What Do You See?* by Bill Martin Jr. allow students to join in and practice fluency in a fun, interactive way.

Example of Fluent Reading in Action

Let's say you're reading the classic story *The Three Billy Goats Gruff.* As you begin, set the tone:

"Once upon a time, there were three billy goats who lived in a valley."

- Read this opening sentence slowly, with a calm tone, emphasizing "three billy goats."

When the troll appears, change your voice dramatically:

"Who's that *trip-trapping* over my bridge?" roared the troll.

- Use a deep, loud voice to capture the troll's menace.

Finally, end with excitement:

"And the big billy goat butted the troll right off the bridge! Splash!"

- Increase your volume and quicken your pace for dramatic effect, making the moment thrilling.

The Ripple Effect of Fluent Reading

Modeling fluent reading daily has a ripple effect. Students begin to mimic what they hear, improving their own fluency. They also gain a greater appreciation for stories and language, fueling their motivation to read independently.

Consider the long-term impact of modeling. When students regularly experience fluent reading, they internalize the nuances of language. This leads to improved comprehension, vocabulary growth, and the confidence to tackle more complex texts.

Conclusion

Fluent reading is an art, and teachers are the artists who inspire their students to create their own masterpieces. By dedicating time each day to modeling fluent reading, you equip students with the tools they need to become confident, expressive readers. Remember, it's not just about teaching them *how* to read—it's about showing them the joy of reading. Start today by picking up a book, setting the stage, and letting your voice bring the story to life.

Lesson Plan 1: Modeling Fluent Reading with Expression and Intonation

Objective

Students will understand how expression and intonation enhance fluent reading and apply these elements during a guided reading activity.

Materials

- A copy of *The Gruffalo* by Julia Donaldson
- Whiteboard or chart paper for key terms
- Highlighter or sticky notes for marking passages

Time Required

30 minutes

Opening Script

"Good readers not only read the words on the page; they also bring the story to life with their voice! Today, we're going to learn how expression and intonation can make reading more exciting and easier to understand."

Define Concepts

1. **Expression**: "Using your voice to show feelings, like excitement, anger, or sadness."
2. **Intonation**: "Changing how your voice rises and falls to match a question, exclamation, or mood."

Activity: Modeling and Echo Reading

1. **Introduction (5 minutes):**
    - Open to a lively passage from *The Gruffalo*.

- Say: "Listen carefully as I read. Pay attention to how my voice changes when I read dialogue or describe something exciting."
- Model reading a passage aloud, such as:

  "Oh help! Oh no! It's a gruffalo!"
  (Raise your voice and quicken your pace to reflect the character's surprise.)

2. **Discussion (5 minutes):**
   - Ask: "What did you notice about my voice? How did it match what was happening in the story?"
   - Write student responses on the board (e.g., "You sounded surprised!" or "Your voice got louder during the exciting part.").
3. **Guided Practice (10 minutes):**
   - Reread the passage and pause after each sentence.
   - Invite students to echo your reading, mimicking your expression and intonation.
4. **Independent Practice (10 minutes):**
   - Assign pairs to practice a short passage. Students take turns reading aloud with expression, coaching each other on how to improve.

Assessment

- Listen to pairs as they practice, noting their use of expression and intonation.
- Provide immediate feedback, highlighting strengths and suggesting improvements.

Intervention

- Work one-on-one with struggling readers, modeling short phrases and guiding them to match your expression.

Enrichment

- Challenge advanced readers to add actions or gestures to their reading, enhancing the performance aspect.

Lesson Plan 2: Phrasing for Fluent Reading

Objective

Students will learn to group words into meaningful phrases, improving their fluency and comprehension.

Materials

- A copy of *Brown Bear, Brown Bear, What Do You See?* by Bill Martin Jr.
- Sentence strips or index cards with pre-written phrases
- Markers or highlighters

Time Required

25 minutes

Opening Script

"Have you ever noticed how breaking a sentence into groups of words makes it easier to understand? Today, we're going to practice grouping words into phrases that make reading smoother and more fluent."

Define Concepts

1. **Phrasing**: "Reading words together in groups that make sense, like 'the big brown bear' instead of 'the big / brown / bear.'"

Activity: Phrasing Practice

1. **Modeling (5 minutes):**
    - Read a sentence incorrectly: "The / big / brown / bear."
    - Say: "That sounded choppy, didn't it? Now listen as I group the words: 'The big brown bear.'"

- Highlight the grouped phrase on the whiteboard.

2. **Interactive Practice (10 minutes):**
    - Hand out sentence strips with phrases from *Brown Bear, Brown Bear*.
    - Have students underline or highlight phrases, then practice reading them aloud with smooth phrasing.
3. **Group Activity (10 minutes):**
    - Divide students into small groups. Assign each group a page to read aloud with phrasing. Rotate groups to share their passages.

Assessment

- Observe group readings, ensuring students group words naturally and read smoothly.

Intervention

- Work with students individually, using simpler sentences and breaking them into smaller phrases.

Enrichment

- Encourage students to rewrite sentences from a favorite book, focusing on phrasing, and present them to the class.

Lesson Plan 3: Engaging with Predictable Texts

Objective

Students will use predictable texts to practice fluency, focusing on rhythm and repetition.

Materials

- A copy of *Click, Clack, Moo: Cows That Type* by Doreen Cronin
- Rhythm sticks or clapping prompts
- Copies of repetitive passages for students

Time Required

30 minutes

Opening Script

"Repetition helps us get better at reading fluently! Today, we'll use a fun, predictable story to practice reading with rhythm and flow."

Define Concepts

1. **Predictable Texts**: "Books with repeated patterns or phrases that make it easier to read smoothly."

Activity: Reading Predictable Texts

1. **Introduction (5 minutes):**
   - Read a passage from *Click, Clack, Moo* aloud, emphasizing its repetitive structure.
   - Say: "Did you notice how the phrase 'Click, clack, moo' keeps coming back? Let's practice that together."
2. **Guided Reading (10 minutes):**

   - Read a repetitive passage with the class, using rhythm sticks or clapping to set the pace.
   - Encourage students to join in on the repeated phrases.
3. **Partner Reading (10 minutes):**
   - Pair students to take turns reading passages aloud. One partner reads while the other listens for rhythm and smooth pacing.
4. **Group Share (5 minutes):**
   - Groups perform their favorite passage with rhythm and expression for the class.

Assessment

- Observe students during partner and group activities to evaluate their pacing and rhythm.

Intervention

- Use simpler texts with more repetition for struggling readers, providing additional modeling.

Enrichment

- Challenge advanced readers to create their own predictable text or poem, focusing on rhythm and repetition.

These lessons highlight the power of modeling fluent reading and provide students with engaging, scaffolded opportunities to develop fluency.

Chapter 2

The Harmony of Choral Reading

Choral reading is a powerful tool that brings students together in a shared experience of fluent reading. In this strategy, the entire class reads aloud in unison, creating a sense of rhythm, collaboration, and confidence. Choral reading is not only an effective way to build fluency, but it also fosters a sense of community in the classroom. This chapter will explore the benefits of choral reading, outline practical ways to implement it, and provide examples to make it a seamless part of your teaching practice.

Why Choral Reading?

Choral reading combines the safety of a group activity with the benefits of practice. For struggling readers, the fear of making mistakes diminishes when they are part of a collective voice. Simultaneously, it allows all students to hear fluent reading modeled by their peers and teacher.

When students engage in choral reading, they practice reading with proper pacing, phrasing, and expression. The repeated exposure to text in a supportive environment helps build their confidence, fluency, and comprehension.

Key Benefits of Choral Reading

1. **Builds Confidence**
   Choral reading eliminates the pressure of individual performance. Students feel more comfortable reading aloud, knowing their voices blend with the group.
2. **Encourages Repetition**
   Repeated readings of the same text help students recognize patterns, improve word recognition, and gain fluency over time.
3. **Fosters Expression**
   Reading in unison encourages students to focus on tone and rhythm, which enhances their ability to read expressively.
4. **Engages All Learners**
   Choral reading works for diverse learners, including those who struggle with fluency, by providing a supportive, inclusive learning experience.

Implementing Choral Reading in the Classroom

To make choral reading effective, thoughtful planning and execution are essential. Here are practical steps to introduce this activity:

1. **Choose Appropriate Texts**
   Select texts that are engaging, age-appropriate, and suitable for choral reading. Poems, rhymes, and short stories with rhythmic patterns work particularly well. Repetition and predictability in the text are key.
   Example Texts:
   - Poems: "Stopping by Woods on a Snowy Evening" by Robert Frost
   - Short passages from *Charlotte's Web*
   - Song lyrics, such as "This Land Is Your Land"
2. **Model the Text**
   Begin by reading the text aloud to the class. Use appropriate expression, intonation, and pacing to model fluent reading.
   Example: If reading a poem like *Twinkle, Twinkle, Little Star*, emphasize the rhythm and expression as you say:
   "Twinkle, twinkle, little star,
   How I wonder what you are!"
3. **Practice Together**
   Read the text as a class multiple times. Encourage students to follow your lead with expression and phrasing. Start with a slower pace and gradually increase speed as they gain confidence.
4. **Divide into Groups**
   For longer texts, assign specific sections to small groups. Each group reads their part in unison, and the whole class comes together for the final lines.
   Example: When reading *The Three Little Pigs,* assign one group to read the lines of the first pig, another for the second pig, and so on.
5. **Incorporate Actions and Movement**
   Adding hand gestures or simple movements to match the text can make choral reading more engaging and memorable.
   Example: While reading the line "The wheels on the bus go round and round," have students mimic the motion of turning a wheel with their hands.

Examples of Choral Reading Activities

1. **Daily Poem Routine**
   Begin each day with a shared poem. For example, read Shel Silverstein's *Where the Sidewalk Ends* as a class. Discuss the tone and emotion before reading it aloud together.
2. **Seasonal Stories**
   Select texts tied to holidays or seasons. In December, use *'Twas the Night Before Christmas* and read it together over a week, focusing on a stanza each day.

3. **Songs as Fluency Builders**
   Songs are inherently rhythmic, making them ideal for choral reading. Sing-alongs like "Old MacDonald Had a Farm" encourage fluency while being interactive and fun.
4. **Scripted Choral Performances**
   Use simple scripts to turn choral reading into a performance. For instance, adapt the story *The Little Red Hen* into a choral reading script. The class can read the repeated phrases like "Who will help me plant the wheat?" in unison.

Encouraging Individual Growth Through Group Reading

While choral reading is a group activity, it also has a profound impact on individual students. As they participate, students gain familiarity with words, build fluency, and become more comfortable reading aloud. Over time, even hesitant readers begin to shine.

For example, a struggling reader who hesitates over the word "star" might feel more confident as they hear it echoed by the class during choral reading. The next time they encounter the word, they'll recognize it faster and read with greater ease.

Troubleshooting Common Challenges

1. **What if students are too quiet?**
   Encourage louder reading by using a playful prompt, such as, "Let's read this like a group of booming giants!"
2. **What if students are out of sync?**
   Slow the pace and clap out the rhythm of the text together before reading again.
3. **What if students are disengaged?**
   Choose high-interest texts or add a performance element, such as props or dramatic gestures, to make the activity more engaging.

Conclusion

Choral reading is more than an instructional strategy—it's a shared experience that unites the class and builds fluency in a supportive way. By reading aloud together, students gain the confidence to tackle challenging texts, improve their pacing, and enhance their expression. With regular practice, choral reading will not only help students' fluency flow but also create a classroom culture where reading is a joyful, collaborative activity. So, gather your class, choose a captivating text, and let the harmony of choral reading begin!

Lesson Plan 1: Introduction to Choral Reading

Grade Level: 2nd - 4th

Time Required: 45 minutes

Materials Needed:

- A printed copy of the poem *Twinkle, Twinkle, Little Star* for each student
- Large poster or projector with the poem displayed
- Highlighters (one per student)
- Teacher's guide to choral reading techniques

Opening Script (5 minutes):

Teacher says:
"Today, we're going to learn about something called choral reading. Have you ever read out loud with a group before? Choral reading means reading together, like a choir singing together. This helps us read with good rhythm, expression, and confidence. Let's start with a poem we all know: *Twinkle, Twinkle, Little Star*. But this time, we'll read it in a way that makes it exciting!"

Lesson Concepts and Script (10 minutes):

- **Define Fluent Reading:**
  Teacher says: "Fluent reading means reading smoothly, with the right speed, expression, and pauses. It's like music for our ears!"
- **Modeling Fluent Reading:**
  Teacher reads the first two lines of the poem with expression and gestures, emphasizing rhythm and tone.
- *Teacher says:* "Did you hear how my voice went up and down? That's called expression. Let's try it together."

Activity Directions (15 minutes):

1. Hand out copies of the poem and read it together slowly.
2. Ask students to highlight the rhyming words (e.g., *star* and *are*).
3. Read the poem line by line, first as a teacher-model, then as a class.
4. Add rhythm: Have students clap gently while reading to keep pace.
5. Gradually increase the speed and expression as students gain confidence.

Assessment:

- Observe students for engagement, pacing, and expression during group reading.
- Use a checklist to note participation and fluency.

Intervention:

- Pair struggling readers with stronger readers for additional practice.
- Revisit one line at a time, reading slowly with exaggerated pacing.

Enrichment/Extension:

- Invite students to create a simple hand motion for each line and incorporate it into the reading.
- Have advanced readers lead a small group, modeling expressive reading.

Lesson Plan 2: Seasonal Choral Reading

Grade Level: 3rd - 5th

Time Required: 50 minutes

Materials Needed:

- Printed copies of the poem *'Twas the Night Before Christmas* (first stanza only for this lesson)
- Markers and whiteboard
- Holiday decorations or props (optional)

Opening Script (5 minutes):

Teacher says:
"With the holidays coming, let's get into the spirit by reading a famous poem together: *'Twas the Night Before Christmas.* This poem has a great rhythm that makes it perfect for choral reading. Let's practice reading it like storytellers!"

Lesson Concepts and Script (10 minutes):

- **Discuss Tone and Mood:**
  Teacher says: "This poem has a magical mood. Let's think about how we can use our voices to show that magic—soft and slow at first, then faster when the excitement builds."
- **Model the First Stanza:**
  Read the first stanza aloud twice, showing pacing and expression.

Activity Directions (20 minutes):

1. Divide the class into three groups: narrators, sound effects, and performers.
2. The narrators read the poem aloud, while the sound effects group adds soft whispers of wind or jingling sounds. Performers act out simple movements like "hanging stockings."
3. Rotate roles so all students experience each part.

Assessment:

- Use a rubric to evaluate group participation, expression, and teamwork.

Intervention:

- Use repetition to build confidence for hesitant readers.
- Break the stanza into phrases and practice one phrase at a time.

Enrichment/Extension:

- Encourage advanced students to memorize the stanza and perform it solo for the class.
- Have students write their own "holiday-themed" stanza to add to the poem.

Lesson Plan 3: Choral Reading with Movement

Grade Level: 1st - 3rd

Time Required: 40 minutes

Materials Needed:

- Lyrics to *The Wheels on the Bus* (printed or projected)
- Classroom space for movement
- Simple props, such as scarves or hats

Opening Script (5 minutes):

Teacher says:
"Have you ever heard the song *The Wheels on the Bus*? Today, we'll use it for choral reading. But there's a twist—we'll add motions to make it even more fun!"

Lesson Concepts and Script (5 minutes):

- **Introduce Phrasing and Rhythm:**
  Teacher says: "In choral reading, we stay together like a team. Let's clap the rhythm first." (Clap out the rhythm of the song together.)

Activity Directions (20 minutes):

1. Teach the motions for each line (e.g., turning hands for "wheels go round and round").
2. Read and move through the song one line at a time, practicing rhythm and phrasing.
3. Perform the entire song as a class, combining reading and movement.

Assessment:

- Observe for synchronization, participation, and fluency.

Intervention:

- Have hesitant students focus on just the motions first, joining in with reading later.

Enrichment/Extension:

- Ask students to create a new verse for the song and teach it to the class.
- Record the performance for students to watch and reflect on their fluency.

These lesson plans provide a robust approach to introducing and expanding upon choral reading in the classroom. Let me know if you'd like adjustments or additional details!

Chapter 3

The Power of Two: Paired Reading

Fluency isn't developed in isolation—it thrives in collaboration. One of the most effective ways to foster fluency in the classroom is through **paired reading**, where a more fluent reader partners with a less fluent reader. This strategy allows struggling readers to hear fluency modeled by a peer while providing opportunities to practice in a safe, supportive environment. Paired reading not only improves fluency but also builds confidence, strengthens peer relationships, and fosters a classroom culture of collaboration.

Why Use Paired Reading?

Paired reading harnesses the power of peer modeling. When a less fluent reader listens to a classmate read, they gain exposure to proper pacing, expression, and intonation. Repeatedly hearing fluent reading helps students internalize these skills and gradually incorporate them into their own reading.

Additionally, paired reading creates a low-pressure environment. Students feel less intimidated working one-on-one with a peer than when reading aloud to the entire class. This safe space encourages risk-taking, which is essential for growth.

How Paired Reading Works

Paired reading is a straightforward yet highly adaptable strategy. Here's how to set it up for success:

1. **Pair Students Thoughtfully**
   Assign pairs based on fluency levels, ensuring that one student is more advanced than the other. Avoid making the differences too drastic to keep the activity engaging for both students.
2. **Model the Process**
   Demonstrate paired reading before asking students to practice. Show how the more fluent reader models a sentence or passage and how the less fluent reader repeats it, matching the pace, tone, and expression.
   Example: The teacher reads, "The sun was shining brightly," with clear expression and pace. The partner mimics this reading.
3. **Provide a Structure**
   Use a simple, structured routine:

   - The fluent reader reads a sentence or short passage aloud.
   - The partner repeats the same text, mirroring the pace and expression.
   - Both readers discuss the meaning or reread together if needed.
4. **Use Leveled Texts**
   Choose texts that are accessible to the less fluent reader while still challenging enough to promote growth. Passages with predictable patterns, dialogue, or rhymes are particularly effective.

Example of Paired Reading in Action

Consider a second-grade classroom practicing paired reading:

Text: *Sally ran to the store.*

- The fluent reader reads the sentence first: "Sally ran to the store," emphasizing the action in "ran" and pausing slightly after "Sally."
- The less fluent reader repeats the sentence, mimicking the pace and expression.
- The pair continues with the next sentence, discussing tricky words like "store" or "ran" if needed.

Over time, the less fluent reader grows more confident and begins to read with greater ease and expression.

Variations of Paired Reading

Paired reading can be tailored to meet the needs of diverse learners and classroom dynamics.

1. **Echo Reading**
   The fluent reader reads a sentence, and the partner echoes it. This is especially helpful for students who struggle with decoding or pacing.
2. **Simultaneous Reading**
   Both partners read the text aloud together, with the fluent reader leading. This approach helps less fluent readers stay on track and build confidence.
3. **Switch Roles**
   After completing a passage, have the partners switch roles, allowing the less fluent reader to take the lead and the fluent reader to provide support if needed.
4. **Timed Paired Reading**
   Use a timer for short intervals, allowing each partner to practice fluency with a set goal in mind, such as reading a specific number of sentences.

Supporting Struggling Readers in Pairs

While paired reading benefits all students, it is especially impactful for struggling readers. To maximize their success:

- **Offer Praise:** Encourage partners to celebrate progress, no matter how small.
- **Focus on Tricky Words:** Teach partners to pause and discuss challenging words or phrases.
- **Incorporate Visual Cues:** Provide bookmarks or finger trackers to help less fluent readers stay focused on the text.

Example Paired Reading Activity

Text: *The cat sat on the mat.*

- **Step 1:** The fluent reader reads, "The cat sat on the mat," with clear expression.
- **Step 2:** The partner repeats the sentence, mimicking the tone and rhythm.
- **Step 3:** Both students reread the sentence together. The fluent reader pauses to ask, "What does sat mean?" prompting a brief discussion to ensure comprehension.

Benefits Beyond Fluency

Paired reading goes beyond fluency practice—it nurtures collaboration, empathy, and mutual support. When students work together, they build relationships that extend beyond reading. Fluent readers develop leadership and mentoring skills, while less fluent readers gain confidence in their abilities.

Additionally, paired reading can spark a love for reading. Students are often more motivated to engage with texts when they experience success and encouragement in a supportive setting.

Overcoming Challenges in Paired Reading

While paired reading is highly effective, some challenges may arise:

1. **Uneven Participation**
   - **Solution:** Rotate partners frequently to prevent one student from dominating. Provide clear guidelines to ensure both students take turns.
2. **Lack of Engagement**
   - **Solution:** Use high-interest texts and set clear, achievable goals for each pair.
3. **Pairing Struggles**
   - **Solution:** Monitor pairings closely and make adjustments as needed to ensure compatibility and effectiveness.

Conclusion

Paired reading is a simple yet transformative strategy that can significantly improve reading fluency. By pairing a fluent reader with a less fluent one, students learn from each other in a supportive environment. This strategy not only enhances reading skills but also builds confidence, fosters teamwork, and creates a classroom culture where fluency flows naturally.

Whether it's through echoing sentences, simultaneous reading, or discussing tricky words, paired reading gives every student the chance to succeed. So, pair up your readers, provide engaging texts, and watch their fluency flourish—together.

Lesson Plan 1: Introduction to Paired Reading

Grade Level: 2nd - 3rd

Time Required: 40 minutes

Materials Needed:

- Short passage: *Sally ran to the store* (one copy per pair)
- Bookmark or finger tracker for each student
- Timer or stopwatch

Opening Script (5 minutes):

Teacher says:
"Today, we're going to practice a new way of reading together called paired reading. This means you'll work with a partner to help each other become better readers. One of you will read first, showing how to read fluently, and the other will repeat. This teamwork will help us all read with great expression and confidence!"

Lesson Concepts and Script (5 minutes):

- **Define Paired Reading:**
  Teacher says: "Paired reading is like being a reading coach for your partner. The fluent reader goes first to show how the sentence sounds, and the partner repeats it. We work together to read smoothly and understand the words."
- **Model the Process:**
  Read the sentence, "Sally ran to the store," emphasizing *ran* and pausing slightly after *Sally*. Have a volunteer repeat the sentence, mimicking your tone and rhythm.

Activity Directions (20 minutes):

1. **Pair Students:** Pair a fluent reader with a less fluent reader.
2. **Practice Paired Reading:**
   - Partner A (fluent reader) reads a sentence aloud.
   - Partner B repeats the sentence, copying the pacing and expression.
   - Both reread the sentence together.
3. **Switch Roles:** After completing the short passage, partners switch roles.

Assessment:

- Observe pairs for engagement, pacing, and expression.
- Use a checklist to track if students are taking turns and practicing fluency.

Intervention:

- For struggling readers, have them echo just a few words at a time instead of full sentences.
- Use simpler passages if needed and provide additional modeling.

Enrichment/Extension:

- Encourage advanced readers to add a question about the passage (e.g., "Why did Sally run to the store?").
- Allow students to write their own short sentences for paired reading practice.

Lesson Plan 2: Echo Reading for Fluency

Grade Level: 1st - 2nd

Time Required: 45 minutes

Materials Needed:

- A short rhyming text: *The cat sat on the mat*
- Visual cues: large text projected or printed on chart paper
- Stickers or praise cards for encouragement

Opening Script (5 minutes):

Teacher says:
"Have you ever heard an echo in a canyon? It repeats what you say! Today, we'll try echo reading with a partner. This will help us practice reading fluently, just like when you hear an echo and copy it."

Lesson Concepts and Script (5 minutes):

- **Define Echo Reading:**
  Teacher says: "Echo reading means one person reads first, and the other repeats like an echo. We match the way the first reader sounds—smooth, clear, and expressive."
- **Model the Process:**
  Read, "The cat sat on the mat," pausing after each word for emphasis. A volunteer repeats after you, mimicking your tone and rhythm.

Activity Directions (20 minutes):

1. Pair students and distribute the passage.
2. Partner A reads a sentence or line. Partner B echoes the sentence, mimicking tone and rhythm.
3. Partners alternate lines, continuing through the passage.
4. Celebrate their progress with stickers or praise cards for effort.

Assessment:

- Listen to pairs for clear echoes and appropriate pacing.

- Use a rubric to evaluate participation and accuracy in mimicry.

Intervention:

- Provide pre-recorded audio clips of the passage for struggling students to listen to before attempting.
- Focus on smaller chunks (e.g., single words) for those needing extra support.

Enrichment/Extension:

- Advanced pairs can add gestures or movement to match the words (e.g., miming a cat sitting).
- Ask students to create an additional rhyming line to extend the passage.

Lesson Plan 3: Timed Paired Reading

Grade Level: 3rd - 5th

Time Required: 50 minutes

Materials Needed:

- Leveled text: *The Wheels on the Bus* passage (one copy per pair)
- Timer or stopwatch
- Progress tracker sheets

Opening Script (5 minutes):

Teacher says:
"Today, we're going to challenge ourselves with a timed paired reading activity. This will help us read faster and smoother! You'll work with a partner to practice fluency and track your progress."

Lesson Concepts and Script (5 minutes):

- **Explain Timed Reading:**
  Teacher says: "We'll read for one minute, see how many sentences we can read, and then try to improve. This helps us practice reading fluently and confidently!"
- **Model Timing:**
  Demonstrate with a volunteer, reading a sentence for one minute and counting how many lines were read.

Activity Directions (30 minutes):

1. **Step 1: Pair and Practice**
   - Partner A reads aloud for one minute while Partner B tracks the lines or sentences read.
   - Switch roles.
2. **Step 2: Discuss and Improve**
   - Partners discuss tricky words and how to improve fluency.
   - Repeat the timed reading, aiming to read more fluently.
3. **Step 3: Celebrate Growth**
   - Record and celebrate progress on a tracker sheet.

Assessment:

- Collect progress tracker sheets to assess improvement in fluency.
- Listen for changes in pacing, expression, and accuracy during readings.

Intervention:

- Use shorter timed intervals (e.g., 30 seconds) for struggling readers.
- Highlight or pre-teach challenging words before the activity.

Enrichment/Extension:

- Challenge advanced pairs to add expressive elements (e.g., changing tone for dialogue).
- Allow students to choose their own high-interest text for timed practice.

These lesson plans provide structured, engaging opportunities for students to develop fluency through paired reading strategies. Let me know if you'd like additional customization!

Chapter 4

Rewind Reading: Mastering the Art of Repetition

Repetition is the foundation of mastery. In reading fluency, repeated reading is a proven strategy to help students improve accuracy, speed, and expression by practicing the same passage multiple times. This simple yet effective approach builds confidence as students see measurable progress, reinforcing their ability to read with fluency and comprehension.

In this chapter, we'll explore how repeated reading works, its benefits, and how to implement it effectively in your classroom. By the end, you'll have practical tools and strategies to make repetition an engaging and valuable part of your students' fluency journey.

Why Repeated Reading?

Fluency is not just about reading faster—it's about reading *better*. Repeated reading allows students to practice decoding, word recognition, and phrasing until they can read with ease and confidence. With each reading, their familiarity with the text increases, and they begin to focus less on decoding individual words and more on reading fluently and understanding the meaning.

This strategy is particularly helpful for struggling readers, as it provides consistent, focused practice. Repeated reading builds automaticity, which is essential for freeing up mental energy to focus on comprehension.

The Core Elements of Repeated Reading

1. **Accuracy**
   Repeated reading helps students correct mistakes and improve their accuracy with words they may have misread or stumbled over initially.
2. **Speed**
   With each reread, students develop a natural pace, reducing hesitation and improving their words-per-minute (WPM) score.

3. **Expression**
   As students become comfortable with the text, they can shift their focus to reading with proper intonation, rhythm, and emotion, bringing the text to life.

Implementing Repeated Reading in the Classroom

To make repeated reading effective, follow these steps:

1. **Choose the Right Text**
   Select a short, engaging passage that is slightly below or at the student's independent reading level. Texts with dialogue, descriptive language, or rhythm work especially well.
   Example: A short paragraph like:

   > *The small gray cat climbed the tallest tree in the yard. She looked down and saw the dog barking below. "I'm not coming down yet!" she thought.*

2. **Set a Purpose**
   Before students begin, explain the goal of repeated reading: to improve fluency by focusing on accuracy, speed, and expression.
3. **Model Fluent Reading**
   Read the passage aloud to demonstrate how it should sound, including proper phrasing and expression.
4. **First Reading**
   Ask the student to read the passage aloud at their natural pace. Time their reading and count the number of words they read correctly. Record this as a baseline.
5. **Provide Feedback**
   After the first reading, give specific, encouraging feedback. For example:
   - "Great job reading the word 'barking.' Let's work on the word 'thought' to make it even smoother."
6. **Practice and Reread**
   Have the student reread the passage two or three more times. Encourage them to focus on improving accuracy, speed, and expression with each attempt.
7. **Final Reading**
   Time the last reading and compare it to the first. Celebrate the progress, whether it's faster pacing, smoother reading, or improved expression.

Example Activity: The Cat's Adventure

Step 1: Give students the following passage:

The orange cat loved to explore. One day, he found a butterfly in the garden. He jumped and swatted, but the butterfly flew away. "I'll catch it tomorrow," thought the cat.

Step 2: Have students read the passage aloud while you time them. Note errors or hesitations.

Step 3: Provide feedback, such as, "You read the word 'explore' perfectly! Let's practice saying 'butterfly' smoothly."

Step 4: Students reread the passage two more times, working on accuracy, speed, and expression.

Step 5: Time the final reading and celebrate their improvement. For example, if the first reading was 45 seconds with 3 errors, and the last reading was 30 seconds with 1 error, highlight their growth.

Variations of Repeated Reading

1. **Partner Practice**
   Pair students to take turns reading and timing each other. The partner can provide encouragement and feedback.
2. **Fluency Graphing**
   Have students chart their words-per-minute scores over time to visualize their progress.
3. **Performance-Based Reading**
   After practicing a passage, allow students to perform it for the class or a small group, encouraging expression and confidence.
4. **Use Technology**
   Apps or recording devices allow students to listen to their first and final readings, reinforcing their growth.

The Benefits of Repeated Reading

- **Builds Confidence:** Repeated practice helps students feel more secure in their reading abilities.
- **Encourages Focus:** Students pay closer attention to challenging words and patterns.
- **Develops Expression:** With familiarity comes the freedom to experiment with tone, volume, and rhythm.
- **Improves Comprehension:** As fluency increases, students can better focus on the meaning of the text.

Troubleshooting Common Challenges

1. **"I'm Bored of This Passage!"**
   - Rotate texts frequently and allow students to choose passages that interest them.
2. **Minimal Improvement**
   - Focus on specific goals, such as mastering one challenging word or improving expression, rather than overall speed.
3. **Student Frustration**
   - Keep sessions short and emphasize progress over perfection. Celebrate every small victory.

Lesson Plan 1: Introduction to Repeated Reading

Grade Level: 3rd-5th Grade
Objective: Students will understand the purpose of repeated reading and practice improving accuracy, speed, and expression with a short passage.

Materials Needed:

- Short passage: *The small gray cat climbed the tallest tree in the yard.*
- Timer/Stopwatch
- Fluency recording sheet (to track words per minute and errors)

Time Required: 30 minutes

Opening Script:
"Today, we're going to work on reading like a pro! Have you ever watched an actor rehearse their lines? They practice reading them over and over until they sound just right—clear, smooth, and full of feeling. That's what we'll do with repeated reading. It's a great way to get better at reading, one step at a time!"

Define New Concepts (Script):

- **Repeated Reading:** *"This is when we read the same passage more than once to practice getting better. Each time, we focus on improving how accurate, fast, and expressive we are."*
- **Accuracy:** *"This means reading the words correctly."*
- **Speed:** *"This means reading at a pace that isn't too fast or too slow."*
- **Expression:** *"This means making your reading sound interesting, like you're telling a story to someone."*

Activity Directions:

1. **Model Reading:** Read the passage aloud, showing accuracy, speed, and expression.
2. **First Reading:** Have students read the passage aloud while you time them. Record their time and note any errors.
3. **Feedback:** Provide specific, encouraging feedback. Example: *"Great job reading 'climbed.' Let's work on saying 'tallest' smoothly next time."*

4. **Reread:** Students reread the passage two more times, focusing on your feedback.
5. **Final Reading:** Time their last reading and compare it to their first attempt.

Assessment:

- Compare words-per-minute and error counts from the first and final readings.
- Note improvements in accuracy, speed, or expression.

Intervention:

- Use shorter passages for struggling readers.
- Focus on mastering just one element (accuracy, speed, or expression) at a time.

Enrichment/Extension:

- Allow advanced readers to perform the passage dramatically for the class or record themselves for peer feedback.

Lesson Plan 2: Partner Practice with Fluency Graphing

Objective: Students will practice repeated reading with a partner and graph their progress over time.

Materials Needed:

- Short passage: *The orange cat loved to explore.*
- Fluency graph templates
- Timer/Stopwatch

Time Required: 30 minutes

Opening Script:
"Did you know that every athlete has a coach and a teammate who helps them practice? Today, you'll be each other's teammates as we practice reading fluently. You'll time each other, give feedback, and see how much you can improve!"

Define New Concepts (Script):

- **Fluency Graphing:** *"This is when we chart our progress to see how much faster and smoother we're getting with reading."*

Activity Directions:

1. **Partner Up:** Students pair up.
2. **First Reading:** One partner reads the passage aloud while the other times them and records errors.
3. **Feedback:** Partners give specific feedback. Example: *"Let's work on reading 'butterfly' without pausing."*
4. **Practice and Reread:** The reader rereads the passage twice more while the partner records progress.
5. **Graph Progress:** Partners use their fluency graph to plot words-per-minute scores for each attempt.
6. **Switch Roles:** Repeat the process with the other partner.

Assessment:

- Review fluency graphs for growth in words per minute and reduced errors.

Intervention:

- Pair struggling students with a peer tutor or teacher. Use shorter passages or assist with decoding tricky words.

Enrichment/Extension:

- Challenge students to write a short passage for their partner to read.

Lesson Plan 3: Performance-Based Repeated Reading

Objective: Students will practice repeated reading and perform a passage to demonstrate accuracy, speed, and expression.

Materials Needed:

- Short passage with dialogue: *The small gray cat climbed the tallest tree in the yard. She looked down and saw the dog barking below. "I'm not coming down yet!" she thought.*
- Timer/Stopwatch

Time Required: 30 minutes

Opening Script:
"Imagine you're preparing to perform on stage. How would you make your words come alive so your audience is amazed? That's what we'll do with repeated reading today!"

Define New Concepts (Script):

- **Performance Reading:** *"This is when you read a passage aloud for an audience, using your best expression and fluency."*

Activity Directions:

1. **Model Reading:** Read the passage dramatically, emphasizing expression.
2. **First Reading:** Students read the passage quietly to themselves, then aloud to you or a partner.
3. **Feedback:** Provide specific feedback on expression and pacing.
4. **Reread:** Students practice the passage twice more, refining their performance.
5. **Perform:** Students perform the passage for a small group or class.

Assessment:

- Evaluate performances using a rubric for accuracy, speed, and expression.

Intervention:

- Provide extra modeling or practice with shorter passages.

Enrichment/Extension:

- Have advanced students add gestures or props to enhance their performance.

Conclusion

Repeated reading transforms fluency from a challenge into a habit. By practicing the same passage multiple times, students build accuracy, develop a natural pace, and gain confidence in their ability to read expressively. This strategy doesn't just improve fluency—it fosters a growth mindset.

As you implement repeated reading, remind students that progress takes time and practice. Each reread brings them closer to mastery and helps fluency flow naturally. So, grab a passage, set the timer, and watch as your students grow into confident, expressive readers.

Chapter 5

Moving with Meaning: Incorporating Actions and Movement in Choral Reading

Fluency instruction should be more than just reading—it should engage the whole body and mind. Adding actions and movement to choral reading connects the text to physical expression, making it more memorable and engaging for students. Research from the science of reading highlights that multisensory learning, which involves auditory, visual, and kinesthetic inputs, strengthens neural pathways and enhances fluency development.

In this chapter, we will explore how incorporating gestures and movements into choral reading can transform fluency practice into an interactive, dynamic experience. We'll also provide examples of choral reading activities that incorporate movement, encourage individual growth, and address common challenges.

Why Actions and Movement?

Incorporating movement into reading activities activates multiple parts of the brain, helping students process language more effectively. When students pair text with physical actions, they create stronger mental connections to words and phrases. This is especially helpful for younger readers, English language learners, and students who struggle with traditional reading approaches.

Key Benefits of Actions and Movement:

1. **Improved Engagement**: Movement keeps students focused and excited, especially during repetitive reading activities.
2. **Enhanced Comprehension**: Physical actions reinforce the meaning of words and phrases, helping students internalize vocabulary and context.
3. **Boosted Retention**: Gestures and movements create a multisensory experience that helps students remember text more easily.

Practical Strategies for Incorporating Movement

1. **Match Actions to Key Words**
   Assign simple gestures to important words or phrases in the text. For example:
   - For the phrase *"The wheels on the bus go round and round,"* students can mimic turning a steering wheel with their hands.
   - While reading a poem about flying birds, students can flap their arms like wings.
2. **Use Rhythmic Movements**
   Add clapping, snapping, or tapping to match the rhythm of a text. This works especially well with rhyming poems or songs.
3. **Incorporate Props**
   Simple props like scarves, paper puppets, or stuffed animals can make movements more tangible and interactive.
   - Example: While reading *The Little Red Hen,* students can act out planting wheat by pretending to dig or scatter seeds.
4. **Encourage Role-Playing**
   Transform choral reading into a mini-performance by assigning roles and encouraging students to act out their parts as they read.
   - Example: In *The Three Billy Goats Gruff,* students can take turns "trip-trapping" across the bridge while others act as the troll.

Examples of Choral Reading Activities with Movement

1. **Daily Poem Routine with Gestures**
   Start each day with a short poem and assign actions to key lines.
   - Example: For Shel Silverstein's *Where the Sidewalk Ends,* have students gesture "drawing a line" for the word *sidewalk* and "point far away" for the line *beyond the street.*
2. **Seasonal Stories with Acting**
   Choose a seasonal text and incorporate simple movements.
   - Example: For *'Twas the Night Before Christmas,* have students mime hanging stockings, pointing to the moon, or pretending to guide Santa's sleigh.
3. **Songs as Fluency Builders with Actions**
   Use familiar songs and add coordinated movements to enhance rhythm and expression.
   - Example: During *Old MacDonald Had a Farm,* students can act out the animals (e.g., waddling like ducks or hopping like rabbits).
4. **Scripted Choral Performances with Props**
   Turn a simple story into a performance with actions and props.
   - Example: In *The Little Red Hen,* students can mimic planting seeds, kneading dough, and baking bread. Props like a toy hoe or a chef's hat add to the fun.

Encouraging Individual Growth Through Group Reading

While choral reading is a collective activity, it profoundly impacts individual readers. Movement, in particular, empowers hesitant readers by giving them a physical way to participate, even if they are initially shy about vocalizing the text. Over time, their confidence grows as they see fluency modeled by their peers and as their bodies learn the rhythm and expression of the text.

Example: A struggling reader who hesitates over the word "round" may initially rely on the movement of turning a wheel during *The Wheels on the Bus.* As they practice, the action reinforces the word, and they become more comfortable reading it aloud.

Troubleshooting Common Challenges

1. **What if students are too quiet?**
   Use playful prompts to encourage louder participation. For example:
   - "Let's read like we're giants stomping through a forest!"
   - "Let's pretend we're cheerful birds chirping loudly!"
2. **What if students are out of sync?**
   Slow down the pace and use actions to guide the rhythm. For example, clap your hands or tap a drum to set a consistent beat for the group.
3. **What if students lose interest?**
   Rotate activities frequently and let students suggest actions or movements. High-interest texts, costumes, and props can also reignite enthusiasm.

Why Movement Enhances Fluency

The science of reading underscores the importance of active engagement in literacy development. Movement provides a tangible way for students to connect with the text, making reading an immersive, joyful experience. By aligning physical actions with words and phrases, students internalize fluency elements like pacing, phrasing, and expression more effectively.

Moreover, movement fosters a positive association with reading. When students are actively involved, they're more likely to see reading as fun, which motivates them to continue practicing.

Lesson Plan 1: Daily Poem Routine with Gestures

Grade Level: Kindergarten-2nd Grade
Objective: Students will practice fluency through choral reading while using gestures to reinforce vocabulary and comprehension.

Materials Needed:

- Poem: *Where the Sidewalk Ends* by Shel Silverstein (or another short, rhythmic poem)
- Large chart paper or digital projection of the poem
- Space for movement

Time Required: 20 minutes

Opening Script:
"Have you ever noticed how fun it is to act out a story or a poem? Today, we'll make our reading come alive with gestures! You'll see how using actions helps us understand the words and remember them better. Let's use our hands, arms, and even our imaginations to bring this poem to life!"

Define New Concepts (Script):

- **Choral Reading:** *"This is when we all read together as a group, like a chorus singing a song."*
- **Gestures:** *"These are movements we make with our hands, arms, or body to show what words mean."*
- **Fluency:** *"This means reading smoothly, like we're telling a story to someone else."*

Activity Directions:

1. **Introduce the Poem:** Display the poem and read it aloud while the class listens.
2. **Model Gestures:** Assign gestures to key words and phrases. Example:
    - "Sidewalk" – Pretend to draw a line.
    - "Beyond the street" – Point far away.
3. **Practice Together:** Read the poem line by line as the class repeats, using gestures.
4. **Full Choral Reading:** Have the whole class read the poem together with gestures.

5. **Add Expression:** Encourage students to add emotion to their gestures and voices during the final read-through.

Assessment:

- Observe students' participation in gestures and fluency.
- Note their ability to match actions with text meaning.

Intervention:

- For struggling students, simplify gestures and provide more modeling.
- Pair them with a peer buddy for extra support.

Enrichment/Extension:

- Ask advanced students to create their own gestures for additional words or phrases.

Lesson Plan 2: Seasonal Story with Acting

Grade Level: 2nd-4th Grade
Objective: Students will enhance fluency and comprehension by incorporating actions into a seasonal story.

Materials Needed:

- Story: *'Twas the Night Before Christmas* (or a seasonal text)
- Space for movement
- Optional: Simple props (e.g., stocking, flashlight for the moon, small sleigh)

Time Required: 30 minutes

Opening Script:
"The holidays are full of exciting sights and sounds! Today, we're going to read a holiday story and act out some parts of it to make it even more fun. When we use movement, it helps us understand and remember the story better!"

Define New Concepts (Script):

- **Acting Out Words:** *"This means using our body to show what the story is saying, like pretending to hang stockings or point to the moon."*
- **Rhythm in Reading:** *"When we read with rhythm, it sounds smooth and matches the beat of the story."*

Activity Directions:

1. **Introduce the Story:** Read the story aloud, pausing to discuss key actions.
2. **Assign Actions:**
   - "Hung by the chimney" – Pretend to hang a stocking.
   - "Pointed to the moon" – Point up to the sky.
   - "Sleigh" – Pretend to drive a sleigh.
3. **Choral Reading with Actions:** Read the story aloud as a group, using the actions.
4. **Performance:** Divide the story into sections, assigning parts to small groups. Students perform their sections with actions.

Assessment:

- Use a checklist to observe student engagement, fluency, and ability to pair actions with text.

Intervention:

- For struggling students, focus on smaller sections of the text or provide props to make actions easier.

Enrichment/Extension:

- Invite advanced students to create additional movements or narrate the story while peers act it out.

Lesson Plan 3: Scripted Choral Reading with Props

Grade Level: 3rd-5th Grade
Objective: Students will demonstrate fluency and comprehension through a scripted choral reading performance using props.

Materials Needed:

- Script: *The Three Billy Goats Gruff*
- Props: Paper horns (for goats), cardboard bridge, troll mask
- Space for movement

Time Required: 40 minutes

Opening Script:
"Have you ever watched a play or movie? Today, we'll be actors in our own performance of a story! We'll read together, act out the parts, and use props to bring the story to life. You'll see how this helps us understand the story better while practicing reading with expression!"

Define New Concepts (Script):

- **Scripted Choral Reading:** *"This is when we read a story out loud together like we're performing a play."*
- **Role-Playing:** *"This means pretending to be a character in the story, using actions and voice to match the role."*

Activity Directions:

1. **Introduce the Script:** Distribute and review the script. Assign roles (e.g., goats, troll, narrator).
2. **Practice Movements:** Demonstrate actions for key parts:
    - "Trip-trapping" – Walk with stomping steps.
    - "Troll roaring" – Gesture with arms and growl.
3. **Choral Practice:** Read through the script as a group, incorporating actions and props.
4. **Final Performance:** Perform the story for another class or record it for review.

Assessment:

- Use a rubric to assess fluency, expression, and connection between actions and text.

Intervention:

- For struggling students, assign narrator roles or simpler actions. Pair them with a peer for support.

Enrichment/Extension:

- Advanced students can write a sequel to the story or create additional props.

These plans provide a multisensory approach to fluency, engaging students at every level.

Conclusion

Incorporating movement into choral reading transforms fluency practice into an exciting, multisensory experience. Actions and gestures engage students' bodies and minds, creating stronger connections to the text and fostering growth in fluency. Whether it's mimicking the motion of turning a wheel or clapping along to a rhythmic poem, movement adds energy and joy to the reading process.

As you implement these strategies, remember that fluency isn't just about reading words on a page—it's about making meaning, expressing emotion, and connecting with the text. With movement as a tool, you'll see fluency truly flow in your classroom, bringing reading to life for every student.

Chapter 6

Empowering Independence: Fluency Centers

Fluency thrives when students have opportunities to practice skills in a structured yet engaging environment. **Fluency centers**, grounded in the science of reading, provide a hands-on, interactive way for students to develop their fluency at their own pace. By rotating through stations that target different aspects of fluency, students gain repeated practice in an independent, low-pressure setting.

In this chapter, we'll explore the research-backed benefits of fluency centers, practical steps for setting them up, and creative ideas to make each station engaging and effective.

Why Use Fluency Centers?

The science of reading highlights the importance of practice, repetition, and multimodal learning in developing fluent readers. Fluency centers are an excellent way to achieve these goals because they:

1. **Encourage Repeated Practice:** Students revisit fluency skills in varied ways, reinforcing their learning through repetition.
2. **Support Differentiation:** Centers can be tailored to meet the needs of diverse learners, from struggling readers to advanced students.
3. **Foster Independence:** Students take ownership of their learning as they navigate activities and track their own progress.
4. **Engage Multiple Modalities:** Fluency centers incorporate visual, auditory, and kinesthetic elements, activating multiple areas of the brain to strengthen fluency development.

Setting Up Fluency Centers

Creating effective fluency centers requires thoughtful planning. Here's how to get started:

1. **Define Your Goals**
   Determine which fluency skills to target, such as accuracy, speed, expression, or comprehension.
2. **Choose Engaging Activities**
   Select activities that align with your goals and keep students motivated. Include a mix of hands-on tools, technology, and written tasks.
3. **Organize the Space**
   Arrange stations around the classroom, clearly labeling each one with instructions. Ensure students can rotate easily and independently.
4. **Provide Clear Directions**
   Use visual aids, written instructions, or recordings to guide students through each activity. Consider including an example at each station.
5. **Rotate Regularly**
   Allow students to spend 10–15 minutes at each center before moving on to the next. This keeps activities dynamic and prevents boredom.

Example Fluency Center Activities

1. **Whisper Phones Station**
   Purpose: Build self-awareness and accuracy.
   Activity: Provide whisper phones (plastic handsets that amplify a reader's voice back to their ears). Students read passages aloud into the phones, listening to their own fluency and adjusting as needed.
   Example Passage: A short text about a playful puppy:

   > *The puppy ran around the yard. He barked at a butterfly and chased it until it flew away.*

2. **One-Minute Timed Reading Station**
   Purpose: Improve speed and accuracy.
   Activity: Students read a passage for one minute, counting the number of words read correctly. They record their scores and aim to improve with each attempt.
   Tools: Stopwatch or timer, leveled passages, and a progress tracking sheet.
3. **Expression Station**
   Purpose: Enhance prosody (intonation, rhythm, and expression).
   Activity: Provide dialogue-heavy texts, such as scripts or picture books. Students practice reading with different tones and emotions.
   Example: A script with lines like, *"I can't believe it!" shouted the boy,* encourages dramatic expression.

4. **Word Practice Station**
   Purpose: Boost word recognition and accuracy.
   Activity: Use flashcards or a word wall featuring high-frequency words or multisyllabic words. Students practice reading the words aloud, focusing on tricky ones.
   Example Words: butterfly, thunderstorm, discovery, imagination.
5. **Recording and Playback Station**
   Purpose: Build self-monitoring skills.
   Activity: Students record themselves reading a passage aloud and play it back to evaluate their fluency. They can use a checklist to identify strengths and areas for improvement.
   Tools: Recording devices, tablets, or computers with recording software.
6. **Partner Reading Station**
   Purpose: Encourage collaboration and peer modeling.
   Activity: Students pair up to take turns reading aloud. One student models fluent reading while the other practices echo reading.
   Example Text: A short fable like *The Tortoise and the Hare.*

The Role of the Teacher

While fluency centers encourage independence, the teacher's role remains vital. Here's how to support your students effectively:

- **Monitor Progress:** Circulate around the room to observe, provide feedback, and assist where needed.
- **Model Activities:** Demonstrate each station's task before students begin.
- **Differentiate Tasks:** Adapt activities for individual needs. For example, provide shorter texts for struggling readers or more complex passages for advanced readers.

Addressing Common Challenges

1. **What if students get off task?**
   - Provide a clear rotation schedule and use visual or auditory cues (e.g., a bell) to signal when it's time to switch stations.
2. **What if some students finish too quickly?**
   - Include optional "bonus activities" at each station for students who finish early, such as drawing a picture about the passage or writing a sentence with a tricky word.
3. **What if students struggle with independence?**
   - Assign a "station leader" to assist peers and ensure everyone stays on track.

Example Fluency Center Rotation

Station 1: Whisper Phones
Station 2: One-Minute Timed Reading
Station 3: Expression Practice with Scripts
Station 4: Recording and Playback
Station 5: Partner Reading

Students spend 12 minutes at each station, completing all five in one hour.

The Science Behind Fluency Centers

Fluency centers align with research from the science of reading, which emphasizes the importance of repeated practice, immediate feedback, and varied approaches to developing reading fluency. Centers provide opportunities for students to:

- Practice decoding skills in meaningful contexts.
- Receive immediate feedback from peers, teachers, or self-assessment tools.
- Engage in multisensory learning, which strengthens neural connections for fluent reading.

Lesson Plan 1: Introduction to Fluency Centers

Grade Level: 2nd-5th Grade
Objective: Students will learn how to use fluency centers, understand the purpose of each station, and practice fluency skills independently.

Materials Needed:

- Whisper phones
- Stopwatch/timer
- Leveled passages
- Expression practice scripts or books
- Recording devices/tablets
- Partner reading fable (e.g., *The Tortoise and the Hare*)
- Progress tracking sheets

Time Required: 45 minutes

Opening Script:
"Today, we're starting something exciting—fluency centers! These are places where you can practice reading in fun and different ways. Each station will help you become a stronger, more confident reader. I'll show you how each one works, and then you'll get to explore them yourself!"

Define New Concepts (Script):

- **Fluency Centers:** *"These are stations where you'll practice reading skills like accuracy, speed, and expression. Each one focuses on something different to help you grow as a reader."*
- **Rotation:** *"You'll spend a few minutes at each station and then move to the next one when you hear the signal."*

Activity Directions:

1. **Model Each Station:**
   - Whisper Phones: Show how to read aloud into the phone.

- One-Minute Timed Reading: Demonstrate timing yourself and counting words read correctly.
- Expression Practice: Read a line from a script dramatically.
- Recording and Playback: Record yourself reading a passage and explain how to use a checklist.
- Partner Reading: Show how to echo read with a partner.

2. **Practice Rotation:** Allow students to spend 5 minutes at two stations to try them out.

Assessment:

- Observe students' ability to follow directions and engage with the activities.
- Use their tracking sheets to evaluate initial progress.

Intervention:

- Assign a peer buddy to guide struggling students.
- Provide extra modeling for stations with complex tasks.

Enrichment/Extension:

- Advanced students can suggest additional gestures or create their own passages for the stations.

Lesson Plan 2: Focused Fluency Practice

Grade Level: 2nd-5th Grade
Objective: Students will build fluency skills by rotating through all fluency centers independently.

Materials Needed:

- Same as Lesson Plan 1

Time Required: 1 hour

Opening Script:
"Now that you know how fluency centers work, we're going to dive in and practice! Remember, each station helps you in a different way—listen to yourself, read with expression, or even time how fast you can go. Let's get started!"

Define New Concepts (Script):

- **Self-Monitoring:** *"Pay attention to what you're doing at each station. Are you improving? What do you notice about your reading?"*

Activity Directions:

1. **Rotation:**
   - Students rotate through all five centers, spending 10–12 minutes at each.
2. **Track Progress:** At timed stations, students record their scores or observations on tracking sheets.
3. **Teacher Monitoring:** Move around the room to assist and provide feedback.

Assessment:

- Collect tracking sheets to review student progress.
- Observe student engagement and ability to follow station directions.

Intervention:

- Pair struggling readers with a peer or adjust the text level at certain stations.
- Provide additional coaching at the whisper phone or partner reading stations.

Enrichment/Extension:

- Have students graph their progress over time or set fluency goals for the week.

Lesson Plan 3: Fluency Celebration Day

Grade Level: 2nd-5th Grade
Objective: Students will showcase their fluency progress through station-based performance and peer feedback.

Materials Needed:

- Completed tracking sheets
- Station materials from previous lessons
- "Fluency Champion" certificates or stickers

Time Required: 1 hour

Opening Script:
"Today is a special day—we're celebrating your progress as fluent readers! You'll have a chance to show what you've learned at each station and even give each other feedback. Let's make this a fun and exciting day!"

Define New Concepts (Script):

- **Peer Feedback:** *"This means giving kind and helpful comments about what your classmates are doing well and what they could improve."*

Activity Directions:

1. **Station Rotations:**
   - Students revisit their favorite stations to demonstrate their best fluency.
   - Partners or small groups observe and provide feedback using a simple checklist.
2. **Final Performance:**
   - Select a few students to read their favorite passage aloud to the class. Encourage expressive reading.
3. **Celebrate Progress:**
   - Share tracking sheets to show improvement.
   - Distribute certificates or small rewards.

Assessment:

- Use peer feedback checklists and observe student performances.
- Review tracking sheets for measurable growth.

Intervention:

- Allow struggling students to read shorter or more familiar passages. Pair them with supportive peers for feedback.

Enrichment/Extension:

- Advanced students can act as peer coaches, helping others improve their fluency.
- Challenge them to create a short skit or poem to perform for the class.

Conclusion

Fluency centers offer a dynamic, student-centered approach to developing reading fluency. By rotating through activities that target different skills, students gain the repeated practice and confidence needed to become fluent readers. These centers also foster independence, collaboration, and a love of reading.

With thoughtful planning and engaging activities, fluency centers will make your classroom a hub of focused learning and joyful exploration, where fluency truly flows.

Chapter 7

Listening and Learning: Audio-Assisted Reading

Audio-assisted reading is a transformative fluency strategy that combines the power of auditory and visual learning. By listening to a fluent reader while following along in the text, students gain an immersive experience that models proper pacing, expression, and intonation. This strategy is especially impactful for struggling readers, as it bridges the gap between hearing and producing fluent reading.

Rooted in the science of reading, audio-assisted reading taps into the brain's ability to process auditory and visual inputs simultaneously, strengthening neural connections that support fluency and comprehension. This chapter explores the benefits, implementation, and creative ways to use audio-assisted reading to enhance fluency.

The Science Behind Audio-Assisted Reading

Research in the science of reading highlights the role of **modeling** in developing fluency. When students hear a fluent reader, they internalize the rhythm and flow of language. This auditory input reinforces:

1. **Word Recognition:** Hearing words pronounced correctly builds automaticity, especially for unfamiliar or challenging vocabulary.
2. **Prosody:** Listening to expression, tone, and emphasis helps students understand how to read with feeling and intention.
3. **Pacing:** Audio-assisted reading demonstrates appropriate reading speed, giving students a benchmark to emulate.

Why Use Audio-Assisted Reading?

Audio-assisted reading provides several key benefits:

1. **Supports Struggling Readers:** Students who struggle with decoding can focus on fluency and comprehension without the added pressure of reading independently.
2. **Builds Confidence:** Listening to a fluent reader empowers students to replicate what they hear, fostering self-assurance in their own reading abilities.
3. **Improves Engagement:** Audio recordings add an interactive element to reading, making the experience more enjoyable and engaging.

How to Implement Audio-Assisted Reading

1. **Select the Right Text and Recording**
   Choose high-interest texts that align with your students' reading levels. Look for recordings that are clear, expressive, and appropriately paced.
   Example: *Green Eggs and Ham* by Dr. Seuss offers repetitive, rhythmic text ideal for modeling prosody and pacing.
2. **Provide Copies of the Text**
   Ensure each student has a physical or digital copy of the text to follow along as they listen to the audio.
3. **Model the Process**
   Play a short portion of the recording while following along in the text. Pause to highlight the reader's pace, expression, or phrasing.
4. **Encourage Mimicking**
   After listening, have students read the same passage aloud, mimicking the audio's tone, speed, and emphasis.
5. **Repetition for Mastery**
   Allow students to listen and practice multiple times, focusing on improving fluency with each attempt.

Example Activity: *Green Eggs and Ham*

Step 1: Play an audio recording of the first few lines of *Green Eggs and Ham.* Have students follow along in their books as they listen.
Step 2: Pause the audio and discuss how the narrator's voice changes when reading dialogue, such as emphasizing Sam-I-Am's excitement.
Step 3: Ask students to mimic the narrator by reading the same lines aloud. Repeat the process for the next section of the text.

Variations of Audio-Assisted Reading

1. **Choral Audio-Assisted Reading**
   Play the audio while the entire class reads aloud together, blending their voices with the recording.
2. **Echo Audio-Assisted Reading**
   Pause after each sentence or phrase, allowing students to repeat what they've heard in the same tone and pace.
3. **Partner Practice**
   Pair students to take turns listening and reading aloud. One partner listens to the audio and follows along while the other reads aloud, then they switch roles.
4. **Independent Practice with Technology**
   Provide students with headphones and access to individual devices for one-on-one audio-assisted reading practice.

Supporting Diverse Learners

Audio-assisted reading is particularly beneficial for:

- **English Language Learners (ELLs):** Listening to fluent reading supports pronunciation, rhythm, and vocabulary acquisition.
- **Struggling Readers:** Students who find decoding challenging can focus on building fluency and confidence.
- **Advanced Readers:** Listening to complex texts modeled fluently helps advanced readers improve expression and comprehension.

Benefits Beyond Fluency

While fluency is the primary goal, audio-assisted reading also enhances:

- **Listening Comprehension:** Students learn to follow and interpret a story through auditory input.
- **Vocabulary Growth:** Hearing unfamiliar words pronounced correctly aids in vocabulary acquisition.
- **Reading Enjoyment:** Combining audio with text makes reading more engaging and less intimidating for reluctant readers.

Troubleshooting Common Challenges

1. **What if students are distracted?**
   - Use headphones to minimize distractions and create a focused environment.
2. **What if students struggle to keep up?**
   - Slow down the audio or choose recordings with a moderate pace. Offer additional practice for challenging sections.
3. **What if students don't mimic the audio effectively?**
   - Pause the recording periodically to discuss specific aspects of fluency, such as tone or phrasing. Encourage students to practice in smaller chunks.

Example Rotation Using Audio-Assisted Reading

In a fluency-focused classroom rotation, audio-assisted reading could be one station:

Station 1: Audio-assisted reading with *Green Eggs and Ham*
Station 2: Whisper phones for independent practice
Station 3: One-minute timed readings
Station 4: Partner reading with dialogue-heavy texts

Lesson Plan 1: Introduction to Audio-Assisted Reading

Grade Level: 2nd-4th Grade
Objective: Students will learn how to use audio-assisted reading to improve their fluency by following along with a text while listening to a fluent reader.

Materials Needed:

- Audio recording of *Green Eggs and Ham* by Dr. Seuss (or a similar text)
- Copies of the text for each student (physical or digital)
- Headphones (optional for a quieter environment)
- Progress tracking sheets

Time Required: 30 minutes

Opening Script:
"Have you ever listened to a storyteller who made the words come alive? That's what we'll do today with audio-assisted reading! You'll listen to a fluent reader while following along in your book. This will help you learn how to read with expression, the right speed, and confidence. Let's give it a try!"

Define New Concepts (Script):

- **Audio-Assisted Reading:** *"This is when we listen to someone read fluently while following along in the text. It helps us see and hear how good reading sounds."*
- **Fluency:** *"Fluency means reading smoothly, with the right pace, and using expression to bring the words to life."*

Activity Directions:

1. **Model the Process:** Play the first few lines of the recording while following along in the text. Pause to discuss the reader's expression and pacing.
2. **Student Practice:**
   - Play the recording again, allowing students to follow along.
   - After the first listen, ask students to mimic the narrator's tone and speed by reading the same lines aloud.
3. **Repeat:** Replay the passage a second time to allow students to refine their fluency.

Assessment:

- Observe students as they follow along and mimic the audio.
- Use tracking sheets to note participation and fluency improvements.

Intervention:

- Pair struggling students with a peer to provide additional support.
- Use slower-paced recordings or shorten the text for students who need extra help.

Enrichment/Extension:

- Advanced students can create their own recordings of a passage to share with the class.

Lesson Plan 2: Choral Audio-Assisted Reading

Grade Level: 2nd-4th Grade
Objective: Students will build fluency by reading chorally with the audio recording, focusing on accuracy and pacing.

Materials Needed:

- Audio recording of a rhythmic text (e.g., *Green Eggs and Ham*)
- Copies of the text for each student
- Progress tracking sheets

Time Required: 25 minutes

Opening Script:
"Reading together can be just as fun as singing in a choir! Today, we'll practice reading with the audio recording as a group. We'll match our voices to the recording to make our reading smooth, clear, and full of expression."

Define New Concepts (Script):

- **Choral Reading:** *"This is when we read together as a group, like a choir sings together."*
- **Pacing:** *"This means reading at the same speed as the recording, not too fast or too slow."*

Activity Directions:

1. **Introduce Choral Reading:** Play a short portion of the recording and have students listen for pacing and expression.
2. **Choral Practice:** Play the audio again while the whole class reads aloud together.
3. **Refinement:** Replay the recording and focus on matching the recording's tone and speed.
4. **Celebrate Progress:** Pause to highlight how well the group is improving with each repetition.

Assessment:

- Listen for improvements in accuracy, pacing, and group synchronization.
- Use tracking sheets to note overall progress.

Intervention:

- For students struggling to keep up, allow them to listen and read silently until they feel comfortable joining in.

Enrichment/Extension:

- Have advanced students lead a line or phrase of the choral reading to model fluency for their peers.

Lesson Plan 3: Independent Audio-Assisted Reading with Technology

Grade Level: 2nd-5th Grade
Objective: Students will independently practice fluency using audio recordings and progress tracking tools.

Materials Needed:

- Individual devices with audio recordings of selected texts
- Headphones
- Copies of the text for each student
- Fluency checklist (to evaluate expression, pacing, and accuracy)

Time Required: 40 minutes

Opening Script:
"Today, you'll get to practice fluency on your own using audio recordings. This is your chance to listen, read, and improve at your own pace. Remember, each time you practice, you'll get better at sounding like the fluent reader you're hearing!"

Define New Concepts (Script):

- **Independent Practice:** *"This means working on your own to build your skills. You'll listen, follow along, and then read the text aloud by yourself."*
- **Checklist for Fluency:** *"This is a tool to help you evaluate how you're doing. You'll check for things like expression, pacing, and accuracy."*

Activity Directions:

1. **Set Up:** Provide each student with headphones, a device, and a copy of the text.
2. **Listen and Read:** Students listen to the audio while following along.
3. **Practice Reading Aloud:** After listening, students read the passage aloud, mimicking the audio.
4. **Evaluate:** Students use a checklist to assess their own fluency or record themselves for playback.

Assessment:

- Review fluency checklists and recordings for accuracy, pacing, and expression.
- Observe students' independent practice and engagement.

Intervention:

- For students struggling to mimic the audio, provide smaller chunks of text to focus on.
- Allow them to replay the audio as many times as needed.

Enrichment/Extension:

- Advanced students can record their own audio versions of a passage and share them with peers for feedback.

These lesson plans provide a structured approach to audio-assisted reading, supporting fluency development for diverse learners.

Conclusion

Audio-assisted reading is a powerful tool for developing fluency. By combining listening and reading, students gain a deeper understanding of how fluent reading sounds and feels. This strategy not only improves accuracy, speed, and expression but also builds confidence and fosters a love for reading.

Whether students are listening to a classic like *Green Eggs and Ham* or exploring a new story, the pairing of audio and text creates a dynamic, engaging experience where fluency truly flows. With the right tools, guidance, and practice, your students can transform into confident, expressive readers, one story at a time.

Chapter 8

The Race for Fluency: Timed Readings

Timed readings are a high-impact strategy for developing fluency, combining focused practice with measurable progress. By setting a timer and challenging students to read as many words as they can in one minute, this method hones accuracy, speed, and automaticity—all essential components of fluent reading. Grounded in the science of reading, timed readings help students internalize word recognition and build confidence through repeated practice and visible improvement.

In this chapter, we'll explore how timed readings work, why they're effective, and how to incorporate them into your classroom in a way that motivates and empowers students.

The Science Behind Timed Readings

Fluency is the bridge between decoding and comprehension. According to the science of reading, fluency is built when students develop automaticity, or the ability to recognize words effortlessly. Timed readings create a focused environment where students practice this skill, increasing their ability to read words quickly and accurately while maintaining comprehension.

Timed readings also engage the brain's processing system by promoting repeated exposure to text, which strengthens neural pathways for reading. As students track their progress over time, they gain a sense of accomplishment, further reinforcing their motivation to improve.

Why Use Timed Readings?

1. **Develops Automaticity**: Timed readings push students to read quickly while focusing on accuracy, helping them move beyond decoding to fluent word recognition.
2. **Builds Confidence**: Seeing measurable improvement week by week boosts students' self-assurance in their reading abilities.

3. **Tracks Growth**: Timed readings provide concrete data that teachers can use to monitor progress and adjust instruction.
4. **Engages Students**: The challenge of a one-minute timer adds an element of fun and competition, motivating students to push themselves.

Implementing Timed Readings

1. **Choose Appropriate Texts**
   Select passages that align with your students' reading levels. The text should be challenging enough to promote growth but not so difficult that students become frustrated.
   Example Passage: A short paragraph about penguins:

   > *Penguins are birds that cannot fly. Instead, they use their wings to swim. They live in cold places and eat fish from the sea.*

2. **Model the Process**
   Demonstrate a timed reading for the class. Show how to read as quickly and accurately as possible, emphasizing that mistakes slow down progress.
3. **Set Up the Timer**
   Use a stopwatch, timer app, or a simple classroom timer. Set it for one minute, and have students read the passage aloud during that time.
4. **Count Words Correct Per Minute (WCPM)**
   After the timer goes off, count the number of words read correctly. Provide immediate feedback, highlighting successes and areas for improvement.
5. **Track Progress Over Time**
   Use a chart or graph to record each student's weekly scores. Celebrate improvements, no matter how small, to keep students motivated.

Example Activity: Penguins Timed Reading

Step 1: Provide each student with the penguin passage.
Step 2: Set the timer for one minute and have students read the passage aloud.
Step 3: At the end of the minute, count the words they read correctly. Record the score on a progress chart.
Step 4: Repeat this activity weekly, encouraging students to beat their previous scores.

Variations of Timed Readings

1. **Partner Timed Readings**
   Pair students to take turns reading and timing each other. Partners can also provide feedback on accuracy and expression.
2. **Self-Timed Readings**
   Allow students to use a stopwatch or timer app to practice timed readings independently.
3. **Fluency Games**
   Turn timed readings into a game by setting class-wide goals. For example, "Let's see if the whole class can read 1,000 words correctly this week!"
4. **Group Timed Readings**
   Have small groups read the same passage together, timing how many words they can collectively read in one minute.

Supporting Diverse Learners

Timed readings are adaptable for all learners:

- **Struggling Readers**: Use shorter passages or allow extra time to reduce frustration. Focus on accuracy before speed.
- **Advanced Readers**: Provide more complex texts or challenge them to read longer passages within the same time frame.
- **English Language Learners (ELLs)**: Choose passages with clear, familiar vocabulary. Encourage multiple practices before timing them.

Benefits Beyond Fluency

Timed readings not only improve fluency but also:

- **Enhance Focus**: Students learn to concentrate on the task at hand, improving both their reading and attention skills.
- **Build Resilience**: Regular practice helps students persevere through challenges, fostering a growth mindset.
- **Boost Comprehension**: As automaticity increases, students can devote more mental energy to understanding the text.

Troubleshooting Common Challenges

1. **What if students feel pressured?**
    - Emphasize personal growth rather than competition. Frame timed readings as a tool to track improvement, not a race.
2. **What if students aren't improving?**
    - Adjust the text level or focus on building decoding skills. Celebrate small successes to keep students motivated.
3. **What if students are disengaged?**
    - Incorporate high-interest passages, such as topics related to animals, sports, or current events.

Example Weekly Rotation

Incorporate timed readings into a fluency-focused routine:

- **Monday:** Introduce the passage and practice as a group.
- **Tuesday:** Partner practice with feedback.
- **Wednesday:** Individual timed readings.
- **Thursday:** Track progress and discuss growth.
- **Friday:** Celebrate achievements with a class-wide fluency challenge.

Lesson Plan 1: Introduction to Timed Readings

Grade Level: 2nd-5th Grade
Objective: Students will learn the purpose and process of timed readings and practice reading fluently using a one-minute timer.

Materials Needed:

- Short passage (e.g., *Penguins are birds that cannot fly...*)
- Timer/stopwatch
- Fluency tracking sheet
- Whiteboard or chart for modeling

Time Required: 30 minutes

Opening Script:
"Have you ever tried to beat your own best score in a game? Today, we'll do something similar with reading! Timed readings are a fun way to see how many words we can read correctly in one minute. Don't worry—it's not a race against others. It's all about improving your own skills each time!"

Define New Concepts (Script):

- **Timed Reading:** *"This is when you read a passage for one minute to see how many words you can read correctly. It helps you build speed, accuracy, and confidence!"*
- **Fluency Tracking:** *"We'll keep track of how many words you read each time so you can see your progress."*

Activity Directions:

1. **Model the Process:**
    - Read the *Penguins* passage aloud for one minute, counting your words.
    - Show how to track words per minute (WPM) and note any mistakes.
2. **Student Practice:**
    - Distribute the passage and tracking sheets.
    - Students read the passage while you time them for one minute.
    - Count their WPM and note areas for improvement.

3. **Feedback and Reflection:**
    - Highlight strengths (e.g., "You read 'penguins' correctly every time!") and set a goal for the next attempt.

Assessment:

- Use tracking sheets to evaluate WPM and accuracy.
- Observe students' engagement and ability to follow the process.

Intervention:

- For struggling readers, use shorter passages or allow multiple practice rounds before timing.
- Focus on accuracy first, encouraging them to slow down if needed.

Enrichment/Extension:

- Advanced students can use longer or more complex passages.
- Challenge them to add expression while maintaining speed.

Lesson Plan 2: Partner Timed Readings

Grade Level: 2nd-5th Grade
Objective: Students will collaborate with a partner to practice timed readings and provide constructive feedback.

Materials Needed:

- Short passages (e.g., *Penguins, A Day at the Zoo*)
- Timer/stopwatch
- Fluency tracking sheets

Time Required: 40 minutes

Opening Script:
"Have you ever had a coach cheer you on while you practiced? Today, you and a partner will take turns being each other's reading coach. You'll practice reading for one minute, and your partner will help count how many words you read correctly. Let's work together to improve!"

Define New Concepts (Script):

- **Partner Feedback:** *"This means listening carefully to your partner and giving them helpful tips, like slowing down or pronouncing a tricky word correctly."*

Activity Directions:

1. **Explain Roles:**
    - One student reads for one minute while the other times and counts WPM.
    - Partners switch roles after providing feedback.
2. **Practice and Rotate:**
    - Distribute passages and tracking sheets.
    - Have partners take turns reading, timing, and recording scores.
3. **Reflect Together:**
    - Partners discuss improvements and set goals for their next attempts.

Assessment:

- Review tracking sheets to monitor progress.
- Observe partner interactions and feedback quality.

Intervention:

- Pair struggling readers with supportive peers.
- Provide simpler passages or allow teacher-led practice before pairing.

Enrichment/Extension:

- Advanced pairs can graph their WPM scores to visualize progress.
- Allow them to create their own passages for practice.

Lesson Plan 3: Class-Wide Fluency Challenge

Grade Level: 2nd-5th Grade
Objective: Students will participate in a class-wide timed reading challenge, fostering a sense of teamwork and motivation to improve fluency.

Materials Needed:

- Multiple short passages (e.g., animal facts, poems)
- Timer/stopwatch
- Large class progress chart

Time Required: 45 minutes

Opening Script:
"Who's ready for a challenge? Today, we'll see how much we can grow as a class! Our goal is to read as many words as we can together. You'll practice timed readings and add your score to the class total. Let's cheer each other on and see how far we can go!"

Define New Concepts (Script):

- **Class-Wide Goal:** *"This is when everyone's individual progress contributes to the group's success. Each person's effort matters!"*

Activity Directions:

1. **Explain the Challenge:**
   - Set a class-wide goal (e.g., 1,000 words read correctly).
   - Display a chart to track individual and class totals.
2. **Timed Reading Rotations:**
   - Students take turns reading aloud for one minute while others count WPM.
   - Record individual scores on the class chart.
3. **Celebrate Progress:**
   - Pause to highlight milestones, such as reaching half the class goal.
   - Reflect on improvements and celebrate everyone's contribution.

Assessment:

- Use the class chart to evaluate overall progress and individual contributions.
- Note student engagement and fluency growth.

Intervention:

- Allow struggling readers to practice privately before joining the challenge.
- Focus on their improvement rather than the total WPM.

Enrichment/Extension:

- Advanced readers can read longer passages or help with scorekeeping.
- Challenge them to lead a "coaching session" for the class.

These lesson plans make timed readings engaging and effective, fostering individual and group growth while developing fluency skills.

Conclusion

Timed readings are a dynamic and effective way to help students build fluency while fostering a growth mindset. By focusing on accuracy, speed, and progress, this strategy empowers students to take ownership of their learning and see tangible results.

As students engage in timed readings, they'll not only improve their fluency but also develop confidence, resilience, and a love for reading. With a timer and a well-chosen passage, you can unlock the potential in every reader and help fluency flow in your classroom.

Chapter 9

Mirroring Mastery: Echo Reading

Echo reading is a simple yet powerful strategy that uses repetition and modeling to develop reading fluency. By having students repeat after a fluent reader, they gain a firsthand experience of proper pacing, intonation, and expression. This approach is especially beneficial for emerging readers, English Language Learners (ELLs), and struggling readers, as it provides a clear model to follow and reduces the pressure of independent reading.

Grounded in the science of reading, echo reading supports fluency by strengthening the brain's ability to process language patterns and connect spoken and written words. This chapter explores how echo reading works, why it's effective, and how to implement it successfully in your classroom.

The Science Behind Echo Reading

The science of reading highlights the importance of modeling for developing fluency. When students hear a fluent reader, they internalize the rhythm and flow of language, which helps them replicate these patterns in their own reading. Echo reading builds neural pathways that strengthen the connection between decoding (recognizing words) and prosody (reading with expression).

Echo reading also supports auditory processing skills, which are essential for understanding how spoken language corresponds to written text. By repeating sentences, students practice blending sounds, recognizing sight words, and grouping words into meaningful phrases.

Why Use Echo Reading?

1. **Models Fluency**: Students hear fluent reading modeled in real time, helping them understand how to read with accuracy and expression.
2. **Reduces Pressure**: Echo reading provides a low-stakes environment where students can practice without fear of making mistakes.
3. **Supports Diverse Learners**: This strategy is particularly effective for ELLs and struggling readers who benefit from auditory reinforcement.

4. **Improves Confidence**: By mimicking a fluent reader, students gradually build their own fluency and self-assurance.

Implementing Echo Reading

1. **Select an Engaging Text**
   Choose a passage that is short, engaging, and appropriate for your students' reading level. Dialogue, poetry, or repetitive text works particularly well.
   Example Passage:

   The dog barked loudly at the stranger. "Go away!" he seemed to say.

2. **Model Fluent Reading**
   Read the passage aloud, demonstrating proper pacing, expression, and intonation. Pause briefly after each sentence or phrase.
3. **Have Students Repeat**
   Ask students to repeat the sentence or phrase exactly as you read it. Encourage them to mimic your tone, speed, and expression.
4. **Provide Feedback**
   Offer immediate, positive feedback, such as:
   - "Great job pausing at the comma!"
   - "I love how you used an excited tone just like I did!"
5. **Practice in Small Chunks**
   Break longer texts into smaller sections. Focus on one sentence or phrase at a time before moving on to the next.

Example Activity: Echo Reading with a Short Story

Text: *The Three Little Pigs*

- Teacher: "The first little pig built a house of straw."
- Students (in unison): "The first little pig built a house of straw."
- Teacher: "But the wolf blew it down!" (dramatic tone)
- Students: "But the wolf blew it down!" (imitating dramatic tone)

As students become more confident, increase the length of the sentences or phrases they repeat.

Variations of Echo Reading

1. **Group Echo Reading**
   Have the entire class echo your reading in unison. This builds confidence, especially for hesitant readers.
2. **Partner Echo Reading**
   Pair students to take turns modeling and echoing each other. This peer interaction reinforces learning and builds collaboration.
3. **Interactive Echo Reading**
   Use props or visuals to make echo reading more engaging. For example, hold up a picture of a barking dog while reading the line, "The dog barked loudly at the stranger."
4. **Echo Reading with Technology**
   Record your reading and allow students to listen and echo at their own pace. This is especially useful for independent practice.

Supporting Diverse Learners

Echo reading is adaptable to meet the needs of all learners:

- **Struggling Readers**: Focus on short, simple sentences to build confidence and avoid overwhelming them.
- **English Language Learners (ELLs)**: Use texts with clear, simple language and emphasize pronunciation and rhythm.
- **Advanced Readers**: Challenge students to echo longer passages or practice varying their tone and expression.

Benefits Beyond Fluency

While echo reading is primarily a fluency-building strategy, it also supports:

- **Comprehension**: Repeating sentences helps students internalize the meaning and structure of the text.
- **Vocabulary Development**: Hearing and repeating new words reinforces their pronunciation and meaning.
- **Listening Skills**: Students learn to focus on auditory input and replicate it accurately.

Troubleshooting Common Challenges

1. **What if students aren't engaged?**
   - Choose high-interest texts or add dramatic expressions to make the activity more exciting.
2. **What if students struggle to mimic fluency?**
   - Slow down your pace and focus on one skill at a time, such as pausing at punctuation or emphasizing key words.
3. **What if students are shy?**
   - Begin with group echo reading to build confidence before moving to smaller groups or individual practice.

Incorporating Echo Reading into Daily Routines

Echo reading is versatile and can be used in various classroom routines:

- **Morning Meetings**: Read a daily poem or inspirational quote and have students echo it.
- **Small Group Instruction**: Use echo reading to introduce new vocabulary or practice challenging passages.
- **Intervention Sessions**: Focus on echo reading with struggling readers to provide targeted fluency support.

Lesson Plan 1: Introduction to Echo Reading

Grade Level: 1st-3rd Grade
Objective: Students will learn the purpose and process of echo reading and practice mimicking fluency through teacher-led modeling.

Materials Needed:

- Short passage: *The dog barked loudly at the stranger. "Go away!" he seemed to say.*
- Visual aids (e.g., picture of a barking dog or a comic illustration)
- Whiteboard for teacher modeling

Time Required: 30 minutes

Opening Script:
"Have you ever heard someone read a story in a way that made it come alive? Today, we're going to practice echo reading, which is a way to learn fluent reading by repeating after me. It's like playing a game where you copy exactly what you hear, using the same tone, speed, and expression. Let's get started!"

Define New Concepts (Script):

- **Echo Reading:** *"Echo reading means listening to someone read fluently and then repeating what they said. It helps us learn how to read smoothly and with expression."*
- **Fluency:** *"This means reading like you're talking to someone, not too fast, not too slow, and with the right emotions."*

Activity Directions:

1. **Model Reading:**
   - Read the passage aloud, demonstrating clear pacing and expression.
   - Show a picture of a barking dog to connect visuals to the text.
2. **Echo Practice:**
   - Read the first sentence aloud: *"The dog barked loudly at the stranger."*
   - Have students repeat the sentence in unison, mimicking your tone.
   - Continue with the next sentence: *"'Go away!' he seemed to say."*
3. **Chunk Practice:**

    - Break the passage into smaller phrases for students to repeat. Gradually combine phrases as they grow more confident.
4. **Feedback:**
    - Provide positive feedback, such as, *"Great job matching my excited tone for 'Go away!'"*

Assessment:

- Observe students' ability to mimic tone, pacing, and expression.
- Note individual participation and improvement during the activity.

Intervention:

- For struggling students, slow the pace and focus on shorter sentences. Repeat phrases as needed.

Enrichment/Extension:

- Advanced students can lead the class in echo reading or try reading the passage solo.

Lesson Plan 2: Partner Echo Reading

Grade Level: 1st-5th Grade
Objective: Students will practice fluency through partner echo reading, alternating roles as reader and echoer.

Materials Needed:

- Short text: A dialogue-rich passage such as a short fable or excerpt from *The Three Little Pigs*
- Visual aids or props related to the text

Time Required: 40 minutes

Opening Script:
"Today, you'll work with a partner to practice echo reading. One of you will read like a storyteller, and the other will be the echo. This is a great way to learn from each other and practice reading smoothly and with expression!"

Define New Concepts (Script):

- **Partner Echo Reading:** *"This is when you take turns reading a sentence or phrase, and your partner repeats it just like you read it."*
- **Modeling:** *"When it's your turn to read first, you're showing your partner how to sound fluent and expressive."*

Activity Directions:

1. **Model Partner Reading:**
   - With a student volunteer, demonstrate how one partner reads a sentence and the other echoes it.
   - Example: *"The first little pig built a house of straw." Echo: "The first little pig built a house of straw."*
2. **Partner Practice:**
   - Students pair up and take turns reading and echoing sentences.
   - Use the same dialogue-rich text to emphasize expression.
3. **Rotate Roles:**

   - After finishing one section of the text, partners switch roles.
4. **Reflect Together:**
   - Have partners share what they noticed about their partner's reading.

Assessment:

- Observe pairs for accuracy in mimicking fluency and collaboration.
- Provide guidance to pairs as needed.

Intervention:

- Pair struggling readers with a supportive peer or have them practice with the teacher before joining a partner.

Enrichment/Extension:

- Advanced pairs can create their own dialogue to practice echo reading.

Lesson Plan 3: Interactive Echo Reading with Technology

Grade Level: 3rd-5th Grade
Objective: Students will use audio recordings to practice echo reading independently, building fluency and confidence.

Materials Needed:

- Recorded audio of a fluent reader reading a passage (e.g., *The dog barked loudly at the stranger.*)
- Devices with headphones
- Printed copies of the passage
- Fluency self-assessment checklists

Time Required: 45 minutes

Opening Script:
"Have you ever wanted to practice reading on your own but still have a model to follow? Today, you'll use a recording of a fluent reader to practice echo reading. This is your chance to match the tone, speed, and expression of the recording. Let's see how closely you can match it!"

Define New Concepts (Script):

- **Technology-Assisted Echo Reading:** *"This is when you listen to a recording of a fluent reader and echo what they say, just like we practiced in class."*
- **Self-Assessment:** *"You'll use a checklist to see how well you matched the recording's tone and fluency."*

Activity Directions:

1. **Set Up Devices:**
   - Provide each student with headphones, a device, and a passage copy.
2. **Practice Listening:**
   - Students listen to the recording once, following along silently in the text.
3. **Echo Reading Practice:**
   - Students listen to a sentence, pause the recording, and echo it aloud.
   - Repeat for each sentence or phrase in the passage.

4. **Self-Assessment:**
    - After practicing, students complete a checklist to reflect on their tone, pace, and expression.

Assessment:

- Review students' self-assessment checklists and observe independent practice.

Intervention:

- Allow struggling students to practice in smaller chunks or with teacher guidance.
- Provide slower-paced recordings for additional support.

Enrichment/Extension:

- Advanced students can record their own fluency passages and share them with classmates for feedback.

These lesson plans offer diverse ways to implement echo reading, supporting fluency development for all learners.

Conclusion

Echo reading is a powerful tool for developing fluency through modeling and repetition. By hearing and imitating fluent reading, students learn how to read with accuracy, expression, and confidence. This strategy creates a safe and supportive environment where students can practice, make mistakes, and grow as readers.

Whether it's mimicking the tone of "The dog barked loudly at the stranger" or echoing a poetic line with dramatic flair, echo reading brings language to life in a way that resonates with all learners. By incorporating this strategy into your classroom, you'll empower students to find their voice and let fluency flow.

Chapter 10

Building Speed and Confidence: Flashcard Fluency

Flashcard fluency is a straightforward and highly effective strategy for developing reading fluency by targeting high-frequency words and common phrases. By practicing with flashcards, students build automaticity—the ability to recognize words quickly and effortlessly. This foundational skill is essential for fluent reading, as it frees up cognitive resources to focus on comprehension and expression.

Grounded in the science of reading, flashcard fluency emphasizes repeated, focused practice to strengthen the brain's ability to process and recall words. In this chapter, we'll explore how flashcard fluency works, why it's impactful, and how to use it creatively in your classroom to engage students and boost their confidence.

The Science Behind Flashcard Fluency

Fluency depends on automatic word recognition, which allows readers to decode text effortlessly. According to the science of reading, high-frequency words—like *the*, *and*, or *was*—make up a significant portion of text, so recognizing them instantly is crucial. Flashcards provide the repetition needed to solidify these words in a student's memory, making reading smoother and more efficient.

When paired with phrases, flashcards also help students practice grouping words into meaningful chunks, an important skill for improving phrasing and prosody (reading with expression).

Why Use Flashcard Fluency?

1. **Builds Automaticity**
   Repeated practice with high-frequency words and phrases helps students recognize them instantly, reducing hesitation during reading.
2. **Supports Struggling Readers**
   For students who struggle with decoding, flashcards provide focused, manageable practice in a low-pressure format.
3. **Improves Phrasing**
   Practicing short phrases helps students group words naturally, improving their fluency and comprehension.
4. **Tracks Progress**
   Flashcards make it easy to monitor student improvement, as you can track how many words or phrases they master over time.

How to Implement Flashcard Fluency

1. **Create or Choose Flashcards**
   Use pre-made flashcards or create your own with high-frequency words, short phrases, or multisyllabic words based on your students' needs.
   Example Words: *the, and, was, because, quickly, jumped*
   Example Phrases: *once upon a time, the big brown bear, in the middle of the forest*
2. **Introduce the Flashcards**
   Begin by introducing a small set of flashcards to avoid overwhelming students. Show each card and model how to read it fluently.
3. **Practice Repetition**
   Have students read each card aloud, focusing on speed and accuracy. Repeat the practice until students can read the cards quickly and smoothly.
4. **Track Mastery**
   Keep a checklist of words or phrases that students master. Once a student consistently reads a card fluently, replace it with a new one to maintain a challenge.

Example Activity: Flashcard Fluency in Action

Step 1: Prepare a set of flashcards with phrases like:

- *The cat jumped high.*
- *She ran to the park.*
- *It was a sunny day.*

Step 2: Show one card at a time. Read the phrase aloud first, modeling fluency.

Step 3: Have the student repeat the phrase, mimicking your pace and expression.

Step 4: Shuffle the cards and repeat the activity, aiming for quicker and smoother reading with each round.

Variations of Flashcard Fluency

1. **Partner Practice**
   Pair students to take turns quizzing each other with flashcards. One student holds up a card while the other reads it aloud.
2. **Timed Flashcard Races**
   Set a timer and challenge students to read as many flashcards as they can within one minute. Track their progress and celebrate improvements.
3. **Phrase Building**
   Combine flashcards to create longer phrases or sentences. For example, pair *the big brown bear* with *ran into the forest.*
4. **Interactive Flashcards**
   Use technology to create digital flashcards with audio recordings of fluent reading. Students can listen to the phrases and then practice reading them aloud.

Supporting Diverse Learners

Flashcard fluency can be tailored to meet the needs of all students:

- **Struggling Readers**: Focus on a smaller set of high-frequency words and provide extra time for practice.
- **Advanced Readers**: Challenge them with multisyllabic words or more complex phrases.
- **English Language Learners (ELLs)**: Use flashcards to reinforce vocabulary and pronunciation.

Benefits Beyond Fluency

Flashcard fluency supports more than just speed and accuracy:

- **Improves Confidence**: Mastering a set of flashcards gives students a sense of accomplishment and boosts their self-esteem.
- **Enhances Vocabulary**: Repeated exposure to words and phrases helps students internalize their meaning and usage.

- **Strengthens Comprehension**: Practicing phrases teaches students how to group words into meaningful chunks, improving their understanding of text.

Troubleshooting Common Challenges

1. **What if students are hesitant or frustrated?**
    - Start with a small, manageable set of cards. Celebrate every success, no matter how small.
2. **What if students lose focus?**
    - Incorporate games, like seeing who can read the most flashcards in one minute or pairing flashcards with movement (e.g., jumping while reading).
3. **What if progress is slow?**
    - Adjust the difficulty of the flashcards to meet the student's level. Focus on accuracy before speed.

Incorporating Flashcard Fluency into Daily Routines

Flashcards are versatile and can fit into various parts of the school day:

- **Morning Warm-Up**: Use flashcards to start the day with quick fluency practice.
- **Small-Group Instruction**: Focus on specific skills, like multisyllabic word fluency, in a small group setting.
- **Homework Assignments**: Send flashcards home for extra practice with parents or guardians.

Lesson Plan 1: Introduction to Flashcard Fluency

Grade Level: 1st-3rd Grade
Objective: Students will learn the purpose of flashcard fluency and practice reading high-frequency words and simple phrases accurately and quickly.

Materials Needed:

- Flashcards with high-frequency words (e.g., the, and, was, because)
- Visual aids for tricky words (e.g., a picture of a cat for "cat")
- Timer/stopwatch
- Fluency tracking sheets

Time Required: 25 minutes

Opening Script:
"Have you ever seen someone who could recognize words in a snap? Today, we're going to learn how to do that with flashcards! Flashcard fluency helps us recognize words quickly so we can read stories more easily. Let's have fun building our reading speed and confidence!"

Define New Concepts (Script):

- **Flashcard Fluency:** *"This is when we use flashcards to practice reading words and phrases quickly and smoothly. It helps us become faster readers!"*
- **High-Frequency Words:** *"These are words that show up a lot in stories, like 'the' and 'was.' If we know them by heart, reading becomes easier."*

Activity Directions:

1. **Introduce the Flashcards:**
   - Show a flashcard and read the word aloud.
   - Have students repeat the word together.
2. **Individual Practice:**
   - Display one card at a time for students to read aloud.
   - Provide immediate feedback, such as, *"Great job! Let's make 'because' even smoother!"*
3. **Timed Practice:**

- Use a timer to see how many cards each student can read correctly in 30 seconds.
- Repeat the activity, encouraging students to beat their own score.

4. **Reflection:**
   - Discuss how practicing helped them get faster and more confident.

Assessment:

- Track how many words students read correctly during timed practice.
- Observe their engagement and accuracy.

Intervention:

- For struggling readers, focus on a smaller set of flashcards and slow down the pace.
- Use visual aids to reinforce tricky words.

Enrichment/Extension:

- Challenge advanced students with multisyllabic words or phrases.

Lesson Plan 2: Partner Practice with Flashcard Fluency

Grade Level: 2nd-4th Grade
Objective: Students will collaborate with a partner to practice flashcard fluency, improving accuracy and confidence through peer feedback.

Materials Needed:

- Flashcards with short phrases (e.g., *the big brown bear, ran to the park*)
- Fluency tracking sheets
- Timer/stopwatch

Time Required: 35 minutes

Opening Script:
"Reading with a partner is like having a coach to cheer you on! Today, you'll practice reading flashcards with a partner. You'll take turns helping each other read smoothly and quickly. Let's work together to improve!"

Define New Concepts (Script):

- **Partner Practice:** *"This is when you take turns reading and listening. Your partner helps you by giving feedback, like saying, 'Great job with that phrase!'"*
- **Phrasing:** *"This means grouping words together naturally, like 'in the park' or 'the big bear.' It makes reading sound smoother."*

Activity Directions:

1. **Explain Roles:**
   - One student holds up a flashcard while the other reads it aloud.
   - Partners switch roles after 5-10 cards.
2. **Timed Practice:**
   - Students use a timer to see how many cards their partner can read in one minute.
   - Record scores and encourage improvement.
3. **Feedback:**
   - Teach partners to give positive feedback, such as, *"I liked how you said 'the big brown bear' smoothly!"*

Assessment:

- Review tracking sheets for progress.
- Observe partner interactions and ability to provide feedback.

Intervention:

- Pair struggling readers with a peer mentor or teacher.
- Use simpler phrases or single words for extra practice.

Enrichment/Extension:

- Advanced pairs can create their own flashcards with more complex phrases.

Lesson Plan 3: Interactive Flashcard Games

Grade Level: 1st-5th Grade
Objective: Students will build fluency through interactive flashcard games that emphasize speed, accuracy, and phrasing.

Materials Needed:

- Flashcards with words and phrases
- Timer/stopwatch
- Game setup: A "path" of flashcards on the floor or a stack for a quiz-style game

Time Required: 40 minutes

Opening Script:
"Who's ready for some fun with flashcards? Today, we're turning fluency practice into a game. You'll race to read flashcards quickly and smoothly while having a blast! Let's see how many words we can master together!"

Define New Concepts (Script):

- **Fluency Games:** *"These are activities where we practice reading quickly and smoothly while having fun. The goal is to get better each time!"*

Activity Directions:

1. **Game 1: Flashcard Path Race:**
    - Arrange flashcards in a path on the floor.
    - Students walk along the path, reading each card aloud as they step on it.
    - Use a timer to see how quickly they can complete the path.
2. **Game 2: Flashcard Stack Quiz:**
    - Create a stack of flashcards.
    - Students draw a card, read it aloud, and earn a point for each correct word or phrase.
    - The student with the most points wins.
3. **Reflection:**
    - Discuss how playing the games helped them improve their fluency.

Assessment:

- Track how many cards each student reads correctly during the games.
- Observe their enthusiasm and fluency progress.

Intervention:

- For struggling students, provide simpler cards and encourage teamwork during the games.

Enrichment/Extension:

- Advanced students can compete in a speed round or write new phrases for the game.

These plans incorporate flashcard fluency in engaging, effective ways, supporting diverse learners while building speed, accuracy, and confidence.

Conclusion

Flashcard fluency is a simple yet powerful strategy for developing reading fluency. By practicing high-frequency words and short phrases, students build the automaticity they need to become confident, fluent readers. With consistent practice and creative variations, flashcards can transform fluency practice into an engaging and rewarding experience.

Whether students are mastering phrases like "the big brown bear" or racing to beat their own speed records, flashcard fluency ensures that every word counts on the journey toward fluency. Let the cards lead the way, and watch fluency flow in your classroom.

Chapter 11

Piecing It Together: Sentence Scrambles

Sentence scrambles offer an engaging way to develop reading fluency and comprehension by combining problem-solving with oral practice. In this activity, students are presented with scrambled words or phrases and tasked with rearranging them into meaningful sentences. By doing so, they strengthen their understanding of sentence structure, improve their decoding skills, and practice reading fluently once the sentence is correctly formed.

Grounded in the science of reading, sentence scrambles support fluency by emphasizing syntax (how words are ordered to form sentences) and building automaticity with word recognition. This chapter explores how sentence scrambles work, their benefits, and practical ways to use them effectively in the classroom.

The Science Behind Sentence Scrambles

The science of reading highlights the importance of syntax and oral practice in developing fluency. Fluent readers not only recognize words automatically but also understand how words fit together to convey meaning. Sentence scrambles promote this understanding by encouraging students to actively think about word order and how punctuation, grammar, and meaning influence fluency.

Additionally, reading the reordered sentences aloud helps students internalize the rhythm and flow of language, reinforcing prosody (expression and intonation).

Why Use Sentence Scrambles?

1. **Builds Fluency and Accuracy**
   Rearranging words requires students to carefully analyze word relationships, which enhances their fluency and comprehension when reading aloud.

2. **Supports Syntax and Grammar Awareness**
   Sentence scrambles teach students how word order affects meaning, helping them develop stronger writing and reading skills.
3. **Encourages Engagement**
   The puzzle-like nature of sentence scrambles keeps students engaged, making fluency practice feel like a fun challenge.
4. **Strengthens Vocabulary**
   Students encounter new words in context, improving both their vocabulary and their ability to decode unfamiliar words.

How to Implement Sentence Scrambles

1. **Prepare the Sentences**
   Select sentences that are appropriate for your students' reading levels. Start with simple sentences and gradually increase complexity.
   Example Sentence: "Sally went to the store."
   Scrambled Version: "went store the Sally to."
2. **Provide Context**
   To help students understand the sentence's meaning, introduce the sentence topic or connect it to a story or discussion.
3. **Guide Students Through Rearranging**
   Have students work individually, in pairs, or in small groups to unscramble the sentence. Provide clues, such as asking, "What word might come first?"
4. **Practice Reading Aloud**
   Once students have reordered the sentence, have them read it aloud fluently, focusing on proper pacing and expression.
5. **Provide Feedback**
   Offer immediate feedback on both the sentence structure and the fluency of their reading. Celebrate their efforts and progress.

Example Activity: Sentence Scramble

Step 1: Provide a scrambled sentence:

"to the park ran dog the."

Step 2: Guide students to unscramble it into:

"The dog ran to the park."

Step 3: Have students read the corrected sentence aloud, modeling fluent reading with expression and natural pauses.

Step 4: Extend the activity by asking students to write or create their own scrambled sentences for classmates to solve.

Variations of Sentence Scrambles

1. **Partner Scramble Challenge**
   Pair students to unscramble sentences together. One student rearranges the words, and the other reads the corrected sentence aloud.
2. **Scrambled Paragraphs**
   For advanced students, provide a short scrambled paragraph. Have them unscramble and reorder the sentences, then read the paragraph fluently.
3. **Interactive Technology Tools**
   Use digital tools or apps that allow students to drag and drop scrambled words into the correct order.
4. **Theme-Based Scrambles**
   Tie the sentences to a theme or story. For example, during a unit on animals, use sentences like:
   - Scrambled: "chased cat mouse the the."
   - Corrected: "The cat chased the mouse."

Supporting Diverse Learners

Sentence scrambles can be easily adapted for different learning needs:

- **Struggling Readers**: Use shorter, simpler sentences and provide visual aids, such as sentence starters or word cards.
- **Advanced Readers**: Challenge them with longer, more complex sentences or scrambled paragraphs.
- **English Language Learners (ELLs)**: Focus on sentences with familiar vocabulary and provide extra support with grammar rules and word order.

Benefits Beyond Fluency

Sentence scrambles develop more than just reading fluency:

- **Improves Comprehension**: Rearranging words requires students to think critically about meaning and context.
- **Enhances Writing Skills**: Understanding syntax helps students write clearer, more grammatically correct sentences.
- **Boosts Critical Thinking**: Solving sentence scrambles strengthens problem-solving and analytical skills.

Troubleshooting Common Challenges

1. **What if students struggle to unscramble sentences?**
    - Provide scaffolding, such as giving them the first word or highlighting key clues like punctuation or capital letters.
2. **What if students lose interest?**
    - Add a competitive element, such as timing how quickly they can unscramble a sentence, or make it collaborative by working in teams.
3. **What if students focus only on accuracy, not fluency?**
    - Emphasize the importance of reading the reordered sentence aloud fluently. Model how to read with expression and natural pauses.

Incorporating Sentence Scrambles Into Daily Routines

Sentence scrambles are a versatile activity that can fit into various parts of the school day:

- **Morning Warm-Up**: Start the day with a quick sentence scramble to energize students and activate their thinking.
- **Small-Group Instruction**: Use scrambles to target specific grammar or fluency skills.
- **Literacy Centers**: Include sentence scrambles as a station in your fluency-focused rotations.

Lesson Plan 1: Introduction to Sentence Scrambles

Grade Level: 2nd-4th Grade
Objective: Students will learn how to unscramble words to form complete sentences and practice reading the sentences fluently.

Materials Needed:

- Scrambled sentence cards (e.g., "ran park to the dog the")
- Whiteboard or chart paper for modeling
- Sentence strips or printed word cards
- Timer/stopwatch

Time Required: 30 minutes

Opening Script:
"Today, we're going to solve puzzles with words! Have you ever seen a mixed-up sentence? We'll figure out how to put the words in the right order to make a meaningful sentence. Once we've solved it, we'll practice reading it smoothly, like fluent readers!"

Define New Concepts (Script):

- **Sentence Scramble:** *"This is when words are out of order, and we work to arrange them into a sentence that makes sense."*
- **Fluent Reading:** *"After we put the sentence together, we'll read it out loud with a smooth flow and expression."*

Activity Directions:

1. **Model the Process:**
   - Write a scrambled sentence on the board (e.g., "to park ran the dog the").
   - Think aloud as you rearrange the words: *"The sentence starts with 'The,' so I'll move that word to the front. Then, what makes sense next?"*
   - Show the corrected sentence and read it fluently: *"The dog ran to the park."*
2. **Student Practice:**
   - Provide students with scrambled sentence cards.
   - Have them rearrange the words to create complete sentences.

3. **Reading Aloud:**
   - Once sentences are unscrambled, students read them aloud, focusing on fluency and expression.
4. **Repeat and Reflect:**
   - Repeat the activity with a few more sentences. Ask students to share what clues helped them unscramble the words.

Assessment:

- Observe students' ability to unscramble sentences accurately.
- Listen for fluent reading and proper expression when sentences are read aloud.

Intervention:

- Provide scaffolding, such as sentence starters or visual cues (e.g., capital letters, punctuation).

Enrichment/Extension:

- Challenge advanced students with longer or more complex scrambled sentences.

Lesson Plan 2: Partner Scramble Challenge

Grade Level: 3rd-5th Grade
Objective: Students will collaborate with a partner to unscramble sentences and practice reading them fluently.

Materials Needed:

- Scrambled sentences on strips of paper
- Timer/stopwatch
- Small whiteboards or clipboards for writing

Time Required: 40 minutes

Opening Script:
"Reading is a team effort, and today you'll work with a partner to unscramble some tricky sentences. Together, you'll figure out how to make the words fit, and then you'll practice reading them like fluent storytellers!"

Define New Concepts (Script):

- **Collaboration:** *"This means working together, sharing ideas, and helping each other solve the puzzle."*
- **Clues for Unscrambling:** *"Look for words that start sentences, like capitalized words, or punctuation that ends sentences, like a period."*

Activity Directions:

1. **Explain Partner Roles:**
   - One student rearranges the words while the other checks for accuracy.
   - After each sentence, they switch roles.
2. **Timed Challenge:**
   - Provide a set of scrambled sentences to each pair.
   - Give them 3-5 minutes to unscramble as many sentences as possible.
3. **Reading Aloud:**
   - Once a sentence is unscrambled, partners take turns reading it aloud.
4. **Feedback and Reflection:**

  - Partners provide feedback to each other, such as: *"Great job pausing at the comma!"*

Assessment:

- Observe teamwork and accuracy in unscrambling sentences.
- Listen for improvement in fluency during oral reading.

Intervention:

- Pair struggling readers with a stronger peer for support.
- Offer simpler sentences to build confidence.

Enrichment/Extension:

- Have advanced pairs create scrambled sentences for their classmates to solve.

Lesson Plan 3: Scrambled Paragraphs for Advanced Practice

Grade Level: 4th-6th Grade
Objective: Students will unscramble a short paragraph and read it fluently, focusing on syntax and comprehension.

Materials Needed:

- Scrambled paragraphs on printed sheets
- Pencils or markers for reordering sentences
- Copies of the original paragraphs for reference

Time Required: 45 minutes

Opening Script:
"Are you ready for a bigger challenge? Today, we'll unscramble not just sentences, but entire paragraphs! You'll use clues to figure out the right order and practice reading fluently. Let's see how well we can solve these puzzles!"

Define New Concepts (Script):

- **Paragraph Scramble:** *"This is when sentences in a paragraph are mixed up, and we have to figure out the correct order to make it flow."*
- **Context Clues:** *"Look for clues in the sentences to decide what comes first, next, and last."*

Activity Directions:

1. **Model Paragraph Unscrambling:**
    - Show a scrambled paragraph on the board.
    - Think aloud to demonstrate how to reorder the sentences: *"This sentence introduces the topic, so it must be first. This one adds details, so it comes next."*
2. **Independent or Group Practice:**
    - Distribute scrambled paragraphs to students or small groups.
    - Have them rearrange the sentences into a logical order.
3. **Fluent Reading Practice:**
    - Once paragraphs are unscrambled, students take turns reading them aloud.

4. **Reflection:**
   - Discuss what clues helped them determine the correct order.

Assessment:

- Review completed paragraphs for logical sentence order.
- Listen for fluent, expressive reading during oral practice.

Intervention:

- Provide sentence starters or hints for students struggling with paragraph organization.

Enrichment/Extension:

- Advanced students can write their own scrambled paragraphs and challenge peers to unscramble them.

These plans scaffold the complexity of sentence scrambles, engaging students while building fluency, comprehension, and critical thinking skills.

Conclusion

Sentence scrambles combine the best of problem-solving and fluency practice. By rearranging words into meaningful sentences, students develop a deeper understanding of syntax and grammar while practicing fluent reading aloud. This engaging, hands-on activity strengthens both foundational skills and confidence, making it a valuable tool for any fluency-focused classroom.

As students unscramble sentences like "went store the Sally to" into "Sally went to the store," they not only master the rhythm and flow of language but also gain the skills needed to become fluent, confident readers. With sentence scrambles, fluency flows naturally as students piece the puzzle together, one sentence at a time.

Chapter 12

Building Fluency with Direct Decodable Reading

Fluency grows strongest when built on a foundation of structured, systematic instruction. **Direct decodable reading books**, carefully aligned with taught phonics skills, provide this foundation by offering texts where 90% or more of the content is directly accessible based on the phonics patterns students have already mastered. These books differ significantly from random leveled readers, which may include words or patterns students have not yet learned, often leading to frustration and guesswork.

In this chapter, we will explore the role of direct decodable texts in building fluency, define how they differ from leveled readers, and provide practical strategies for incorporating them into your classroom routines, including independent work, small group instruction, and assessment.

What Are Direct Decodable Reading Books?

A **direct decodable book** is a carefully designed text where students can decode nearly all the words using phonics rules they have already been taught. For example, if students have mastered consonants, short vowels, and consonant-vowel-consonant (CVC) patterns, they might read sentences like:

- *The cat sat on the mat.*
- *Sam ran to the big red hut.*

Direct decodables are sequenced to align with systematic phonics instruction. For instance, students must have fully mastered **quadrant one of Teach BIG phonics** (basic consonants and short vowels) before encountering texts using CVC words. Quadrant three, which includes digraphs like *sh* and *ch*, must also be taught in full before students encounter texts that include these patterns.

In contrast, **leveled readers** often group texts based on readability formulas rather than phonics progression. They may include irregular words, multi-syllabic words, or vowel teams before students are ready to decode them, leading to guessing rather than reading with confidence.

How Direct Decodables Build Fluency

1. **Develops Automaticity**
   Students repeatedly practice decoding words with familiar patterns, increasing speed and accuracy.
   Example Sentence: *Pat had a nap on the bed.*
2. **Reinforces Phonics Rules**
   Direct decodables reinforce phonics concepts taught in class, helping students apply their learning to real texts.
3. **Promotes Confidence**
   When students encounter texts they can fully decode, they experience success, which builds motivation and confidence.
4. **Supports Gradual Progression**
   Each text builds on previous skills, ensuring that students develop fluency systematically without being overwhelmed.

Direct Decodables in Classroom Practice

Independent Work

1. **Daily Reading Practice**
   Provide students with direct decodable books that match their current phonics knowledge. Assign a short passage or chapter for them to read independently, focusing on accuracy and expression.
   Example Book Title: *Pam and the Pig*
   - *Pam sat in the big red van.*
   - *The pig ran up the hill.*
2. **Fluency Graphing**
   Have students time themselves reading a passage and graph their words-per-minute (WPM) each week. This visual progress tracker motivates students and shows growth over time.

Small Group Instruction

1. **Targeted Skill Practice**
   Use small group sessions to practice decoding and fluency with direct decodables that match the group's phonics level.
   Example Activity: Read aloud a sentence like *"Tim had a bad hat."* Ask students to take turns decoding each word and then reread the sentence fluently.

2. **Echo Reading**
   Model fluent reading of a passage, then have students repeat after you. Focus on pace, accuracy, and prosody.
3. **Phrase Building**
   Provide word cards with simple phrases like *"The dog"* or *"ran fast"*. Have students arrange the cards into sentences and read them aloud.

Assessment and Monitoring

1. **One-on-One Fluency Checks**
   Periodically assess students' fluency with a short passage from a direct decodable book. Measure WPM, accuracy, and expression.
   Example Passage:
   - *The sun is hot.*
   - *The dog dug in the wet sand.*
2. **Error Analysis**
   Note any patterns in mistakes, such as misreading digraphs like *ch* or confusing short vowel sounds. Use this data to adjust instruction.

Example Text Progression

Below is an example progression of direct decodable content based on systematic phonics instruction:

1. **Quadrant One: Basic CVC Words**
   - *Pat had a cat.*
   - *The man ran to the big red bus.*
2. **Quadrant Two: Blends**
   - *Brad went to the pond.*
   - *The frog sat on a flat rock.*
3. **Quadrant Three: Digraphs (sh, ch, th, wh)**
   - *Chip had a wish.*
   - *Beth sat on the bench.*
4. **Quadrant Four: Long Vowels with Silent E**
   - *Pete ate a cake.*
   - *The kite is on the lake.*

Supporting Diverse Learners

1. **Struggling Readers**
   Use shorter, simpler texts with fewer words per page to build confidence. Provide additional modeling and guided practice.
2. **Advanced Readers**
   Challenge students with longer passages or sentences that include more complex patterns from previously mastered quadrants.
3. **English Language Learners (ELLs)**
   Focus on simple, familiar vocabulary and pair reading with visuals to aid comprehension.

Troubleshooting Challenges

1. **What if students are guessing words?**
   - Remind them to use decoding strategies and avoid rushing. Provide corrective feedback as needed.
2. **What if progress is slow?**
   - Revisit earlier phonics skills and provide more practice with simpler texts.
3. **What if students lose interest?**
   - Use engaging direct decodable stories with colorful illustrations or relatable characters.

Lesson Plan 1: Introduction to Direct Decodable Reading

Grade Level: Kindergarten-2nd Grade
Objective: Students will use direct decodable texts to practice decoding CVC words and read sentences fluently.

Materials Needed:

- Direct decodable books (aligned to students' phonics knowledge, such as *Pam and the Pig*)
- Whiteboard or chart for modeling decoding
- Fluency tracking sheets

Time Required: 30 minutes

Opening Script:
"Today, we're going to read a special kind of book called a direct decodable book. These books are like puzzles, and the pieces are words you already know how to read! By using what you've learned in phonics, you'll be able to read every word in these stories. Let's practice decoding and reading fluently!"

Define New Concepts (Script):

- **Direct Decodable Books:** *"These are books where almost all the words can be sounded out using the phonics rules we've learned. They help us practice reading fluently and confidently."*
- **Decoding:** *"This means breaking words into sounds and blending them together to read the word."*

Activity Directions:

1. **Model Decoding:**
   - Write a CVC word from the text on the board (e.g., *pig*).
   - Say: *"Let's decode this word. We'll start with the sounds: /p/ /i/ /g/. Now, let's blend them: pig!"*
2. **Guided Reading Practice:**
   - Read a sentence aloud from the text (e.g., *Pam sat in the van*).

    - Have students echo the sentence, decoding each word as needed.
3. **Independent Practice:**
    - Students read a short passage from the book aloud to a partner or the teacher.
4. **Reflection:**
    - Discuss how using phonics helps them read fluently.

Assessment:

- Observe students decoding words and reading sentences aloud.
- Use a checklist to note their accuracy and fluency.

Intervention:

- Provide extra modeling for struggling students. Use simpler words and sentences to build confidence.

Enrichment/Extension:

- Advanced students can read longer sentences or write their own sentences using the same phonics patterns.

Lesson Plan 2: Small Group Fluency Practice

Grade Level: 1st-3rd Grade
Objective: Students will practice fluency in small groups using direct decodable texts, focusing on accuracy, pacing, and expression.

Materials Needed:

- Direct decodable books (aligned to group phonics levels)
- Word cards with CVC patterns and simple phrases
- Timer/stopwatch

Time Required: 40 minutes

Opening Script:
"Today, we'll work in small groups to practice fluency. We'll use books and word cards that match the phonics skills you already know. By reading together, we can help each other build confidence and become fluent readers!"

Define New Concepts (Script):

- **Fluency:** *"This means reading like you're talking—smoothly, with the right speed and expression."*
- **Expression:** *"This means making your voice sound interesting, like when you're telling a story."*

Activity Directions:

1. **Group Reading:**
    - Have students take turns reading sentences aloud from the direct decodable text.
    - Pause to provide feedback: *"Great job with the word 'cat.' Let's work on reading the whole sentence smoothly."*
2. **Word Card Practice:**
    - Use word cards to practice decoding. Ask students to read words individually, then form sentences (e.g., *The cat ran fast*).
3. **Timed Reading:**

  - Have students read a short passage for one minute. Record how many words they read correctly.
4. **Reflection:**
  - Discuss how fluency improved through practice.

Assessment:

- Use fluency tracking sheets to monitor WPM and accuracy during timed readings.
- Observe students' ability to decode words and read fluently.

Intervention:

- Provide smaller groups or one-on-one practice for struggling students. Focus on a few sentences at a time.

Enrichment/Extension:

- Challenge advanced groups with passages containing blends or digraphs (e.g., *Brad went to the pond*).

Lesson Plan 3: Fluency Graphing with Independent Reading

Grade Level: 2nd-4th Grade
Objective: Students will independently practice fluency using direct decodable books and track their progress over time with a fluency graph.

Materials Needed:

- Direct decodable books (e.g., *The Sun is Hot*)
- Timer/stopwatch
- Fluency graphs

Time Required: 30 minutes

Opening Script:
"Today, you'll work independently to practice reading fluently. You'll read a passage from your book, time yourself, and graph how many words you read in one minute. Let's see how practice can help us grow!"

Define New Concepts (Script):

- **Fluency Graph:** *"This is a chart where we record how many words we can read in one minute. It helps us see our progress over time."*
- **Progress:** *"Each time we practice, we get better and faster, even if it's just a little bit!"*

Activity Directions:

1. **Independent Reading:**
   - Assign a short passage to each student.
   - Have them read the passage aloud, timing themselves for one minute.
2. **Track Progress:**
   - Students count how many words they read correctly and plot it on their fluency graph.
3. **Repeat for Improvement:**
   - Have students reread the passage, trying to improve their score.
4. **Reflection:**
   - Ask students to share how they felt about their progress.

Assessment:

- Review fluency graphs to track individual growth.
- Listen to students' reading to assess accuracy and expression.

Intervention:

- Provide simpler passages or one-on-one support for struggling readers.

Enrichment/Extension:

- Advanced students can compare their fluency on different passages or write their own decodable stories to practice.

These lesson plans provide structured, engaging activities for building fluency with direct decodable texts, supporting a range of learners while fostering confidence and skill mastery.

Conclusion

Direct decodable books are a cornerstone of effective fluency instruction. By aligning texts with students' phonics knowledge, these books empower students to read with confidence, accuracy, and expression. Unlike leveled readers, which may overwhelm or frustrate early readers, direct decodables provide a clear path for fluency development, one skill at a time.

As students decode sentences like *"Sally went to the store"* or *"The big dog ran fast,"* they not only master foundational reading skills but also gain the confidence to tackle more complex texts in the future. With direct decodable books, fluency flows naturally, building skilled, confident readers one word at a time.

Chapter 13

Filling the Gaps: Close Reading Exercises

Close reading exercises are a dynamic strategy for building both fluency and comprehension by engaging students in filling in missing words within a passage. This activity requires students to actively think about context, vocabulary, and syntax while maintaining fluency as they read aloud. Rooted in the science of reading, close reading exercises strengthen multiple components of literacy, including decoding, word recognition, and meaning-making.

In this chapter, we will explore the benefits of close reading, practical ways to implement it, and how it fosters both fluency and deeper understanding of text.

What Are Close Reading Exercises?

Close reading exercises involve providing students with a passage that contains intentional blanks where key words have been removed. Students are tasked with supplying the missing words based on context clues, sentence structure, and prior knowledge. Once they fill in the blanks, they read the complete passage aloud to practice fluency.

Example Passage:

- *The ___ jumped over the moon.*
- Missing word: *cow*

Close reading exercises are distinct from standard fluency drills because they require students to engage in comprehension while maintaining fluency. This dual focus ensures that students are not only reading accurately and expressively but also understanding the text at a deeper level.

The Science Behind Close Reading Exercises

The science of reading emphasizes the interconnectedness of decoding, fluency, and comprehension. Close reading exercises support these elements by:

1. **Enhancing Contextual Understanding**
   Students learn to use context clues to determine the missing words, improving their ability to infer meaning and predict text.
2. **Reinforcing Syntax and Grammar**
   Rearranging sentences with blanks encourages students to think critically about sentence structure and the role of specific words.
3. **Building Automaticity**
   Repeated practice with similar patterns and structures helps students recognize high-frequency words and phrases more quickly.
4. **Strengthening Fluency**
   After filling in the blanks, students practice reading the full passage aloud with accuracy, pacing, and expression.

Why Use Close Reading Exercises?

1. **Combines Fluency and Comprehension**
   This strategy bridges the gap between reading words accurately and understanding their meaning.
2. **Engages Students Actively**
   Filling in blanks turns reading into an interactive problem-solving activity, keeping students motivated.
3. **Supports Vocabulary Development**
   Students are exposed to new words and phrases in meaningful contexts, helping them expand their vocabulary.
4. **Encourages Critical Thinking**
   Determining the missing words requires students to analyze the text and consider multiple possibilities before selecting the correct answer.

Implementing Close Reading Exercises

1. **Choose a Text**
   Select a passage that aligns with your students' reading level and current learning objectives. Ensure the missing words can be inferred using context clues.
   Example Passage:
   - *The ___ sat on the ___ mat.*
   - Missing words: *cat* and *red*

2. **Prepare the Passage**
   Remove one to three words per sentence, focusing on high-frequency or meaningful words that challenge students without overwhelming them.
3. **Introduce the Activity**
   Read the passage aloud first, modeling how to use context to determine the missing words.
4. **Guide Students Through the Exercise**
   Provide copies of the passage with blanks and work through the first few sentences together. Encourage students to share their reasoning for each word choice.
5. **Practice Fluency**
   Once the blanks are filled, have students read the complete passage aloud, focusing on accuracy, pacing, and expression.

Example Activity: Close Reading in Action

Step 1: Provide the following passage:

- *The ___ barked at the ___ boy.*
- Missing words: *dog* and *small*

Step 2: Ask students to use the context to determine the missing words. Discuss why *dog* fits better than *cat* in this sentence.

Step 3: After completing the passage, students read it aloud:

- *The dog barked at the small boy.*

Step 4: Repeat with a new passage or allow students to create their own blanks for classmates to solve.

Variations of Close Reading Exercises

1. **Partner Fill-Ins**
   Pair students to work together on filling in the blanks and reading the completed passage aloud.
2. **Thematic Close Reading**
   Use passages tied to a theme or unit of study, such as animals, weather, or holidays.
   Example:
   - *The ___ built a ___ house in the snow.*
   - Missing words: *man* and *small*

3. **Interactive Digital Close Reading**
   Use digital tools or apps that allow students to drag and drop words into blanks or type their answers directly.
4. **Challenge Words**
   Provide several possible options for each blank, increasing the difficulty level.
   Example:
   - *The ___ climbed up the hill.*
   - Options: *dog, cat, fox*

Supporting Diverse Learners

1. **Struggling Readers**
   Use simpler passages with fewer blanks and provide word banks or sentence frames as scaffolds.
2. **Advanced Readers**
   Challenge advanced students with longer passages or multiple blanks per sentence.
3. **English Language Learners (ELLs)**
   Focus on high-frequency words and provide visuals or context to support understanding.

Benefits Beyond Fluency

Close reading exercises improve fluency and comprehension while also:

- **Developing Analytical Skills**: Students analyze text for clues, improving critical thinking.
- **Improving Writing Skills**: Understanding sentence structure through close reading strengthens writing abilities.
- **Enhancing Listening Skills**: When students listen to peers read their completed passages, they practice active listening and comprehension.

Troubleshooting Common Challenges

1. **What if students struggle to fill in the blanks?**
   - Provide word banks or guide them by asking leading questions like, "What word makes sense here?"
2. **What if students lose interest?**
   - Use engaging, relatable passages or add an element of competition by timing how quickly they can complete the exercise.
3. **What if fluency is weak after completing the exercise?**

- Model fluent reading of the passage and encourage students to reread multiple times to improve their pacing and expression.

Incorporating Close Reading Exercises Into Your Routine

- **Morning Warm-Ups**: Use a short passage with blanks as a quick fluency-building activity.
- **Small-Group Instruction**: Focus on specific comprehension or vocabulary goals with targeted passages.
- **Homework Assignments**: Provide close reading passages for additional practice at home.

Lesson Plan 1: Introduction to Close Reading Exercises

Grade Level: 2nd-4th Grade
Objective: Students will use context clues and sentence structure to fill in missing words and read completed passages fluently.

Materials Needed:

- Passages with blanks (e.g., "The ___ barked at the ___ boy.")
- Word banks for struggling readers
- Whiteboard or chart for group practice
- Printed passages for individual work

Time Required: 30 minutes

Opening Script:
"Have you ever solved a puzzle and felt proud of figuring it out? Today, we're going to do something similar with reading. I'll give you sentences with missing words, and your job is to figure out what fits best. Then, we'll practice reading the sentences smoothly, like fluent readers!"

Define New Concepts (Script):

- **Close Reading:** *"This is when we carefully read a sentence to figure out missing words using clues from the text."*
- **Context Clues:** *"These are hints in the sentence that help us guess what the missing word might be."*

Activity Directions:

1. **Model the Process:**
   - Write the sentence *"The ___ barked at the ___ boy."* on the board.
   - Think aloud: *"What barks? A dog! Now let's try the second blank. What kind of boy? Maybe small. So the sentence is: 'The dog barked at the small boy.'"*
2. **Guided Practice:**
   - Provide students with a similar sentence.
   - Work together as a group to fill in the blanks. Discuss why certain words fit best.

3. **Independent Practice:**
    - Distribute printed passages with blanks.
    - Students fill in the blanks individually or with a partner.
4. **Fluency Practice:**
    - Once sentences are complete, students read them aloud, focusing on fluency and expression.

Assessment:

- Review completed passages for accuracy.
- Observe students' fluency during oral reading.

Intervention:

- Provide word banks or sentence starters for struggling readers.
- Read sentences aloud together before students complete them.

Enrichment/Extension:

- Advanced students can create their own sentences with blanks for peers to solve.

Lesson Plan 2: Partner Fill-Ins for Close Reading

Grade Level: 3rd-5th Grade
Objective: Students will collaborate to fill in missing words and practice reading completed passages fluently.

Materials Needed:

- Partner passages with blanks (e.g., "The ___ climbed the ___ tree.")
- Word cards or word banks for optional support
- Timer/stopwatch for timed reading practice

Time Required: 35 minutes

Opening Script:
"Today, you'll work with a partner to solve some word puzzles. You'll figure out the missing words together and take turns reading the completed sentences aloud. It's teamwork with a reading twist!"

Define New Concepts (Script):

- **Teamwork in Close Reading:** *"You and your partner will share ideas to decide which words fit best. Then, you'll help each other practice reading smoothly."*

Activity Directions:

1. **Explain Partner Roles:**
    - One student suggests a word for the blank, and the other agrees or suggests an alternative.
    - Switch roles after each sentence.
2. **Collaborative Practice:**
    - Give each pair a set of passages with blanks.
    - Partners discuss and fill in the blanks together.
3. **Fluency Reading:**
    - Partners take turns reading the completed sentences aloud.
    - Use a timer to challenge them to improve their pacing with repeated reads.
4. **Reflection:**

- Partners share how they decided on the missing words.

Assessment:

- Listen to partners' discussions to evaluate comprehension and reasoning.
- Observe their fluency during oral reading.

Intervention:

- Assign simpler sentences or provide more structured support for struggling students.

Enrichment/Extension:

- Challenge pairs to create a short paragraph with blanks for another team to solve.

Lesson Plan 3: Thematic Close Reading Challenge

Grade Level: 4th-6th Grade
Objective: Students will apply close reading skills to themed passages, improving their fluency and comprehension within a specific context.

Materials Needed:

- Themed passages with blanks (e.g., animals: "The ___ jumped over the ___ fence.")
- Visual aids related to the theme (e.g., pictures of animals or settings)
- Word banks for optional support

Time Required: 45 minutes

Opening Script:
"Today, we're diving into a theme while practicing our reading skills! The sentences are all about animals, and some words are missing. Your job is to figure out the blanks using clues and then read the sentences fluently. Let's have fun exploring while we learn!"

Define New Concepts (Script):

- **Thematic Close Reading:** *"This means all the sentences are connected by a theme, like animals or weather. Thinking about the theme can help you figure out the missing words."*

Activity Directions:

1. **Introduce the Theme:**
   - Show pictures or discuss the theme (e.g., animals).
   - Example sentence: *"The ___ ran through the ___ field."*
   - Think aloud: *"If this is about animals, a horse might run through a green field."*
2. **Small Group Work:**
   - Divide students into small groups and provide each group with a set of passages.
   - Groups collaborate to fill in the blanks, using visuals and context clues.
3. **Fluency Reading Challenge:**
   - Each group nominates one student to read their completed sentences aloud to the class.

   - Focus on fluency, expression, and pacing.
4. **Reflection and Feedback:**
   - Discuss how the theme helped with context and comprehension.

Assessment:

- Review groups' completed passages for accuracy and appropriateness.
- Evaluate fluency during group presentations.

Intervention:

- Offer sentence frames or individual support for struggling students.

Enrichment/Extension:

- Advanced groups can create their own themed passages with blanks for classmates to solve.

These lesson plans provide an engaging and structured approach to close reading exercises, fostering both fluency and comprehension while catering to diverse learners.

Conclusion

Close reading exercises offer an engaging and effective way to build fluency and comprehension simultaneously. By challenging students to fill in missing words and read completed passages fluently, this strategy helps develop critical reading skills while fostering confidence and enjoyment.

Whether it's completing a sentence like *"The ___ jumped over the moon"* or deciphering a more complex passage, close reading encourages active engagement with text, ensuring that fluency flows naturally from understanding. With each blank filled, students grow into confident, capable readers ready to tackle any challenge.

Chapter 14

Speaking with Confidence: Oral Book Summaries

Oral book summaries are an engaging and effective strategy for combining fluency practice with comprehension and oral expression. By summarizing a book aloud, students develop the ability to synthesize key information, organize their thoughts, and deliver their ideas with fluency and expression. This activity not only reinforces understanding of the text but also builds confidence in public speaking and communication skills.

Grounded in the science of reading, oral book summaries emphasize the importance of fluency as an integrated skill that goes beyond reading text—it includes comprehension, oral language development, and the ability to convey meaning.

The Science Behind Oral Book Summaries

The science of reading highlights the connection between fluency and comprehension. True fluency requires not just the ability to read words accurately and expressively, but also the ability to understand and convey the meaning of the text. Oral book summaries bridge these skills by requiring students to:

1. **Comprehend the Text**
   Students must identify the main events, characters, and themes, ensuring they grasp the story's meaning.
2. **Organize Information**
   Summarizing requires students to structure their thoughts logically, focusing on the most important details.
3. **Practice Oral Fluency**
   When presenting aloud, students use expression, pacing, and clarity to communicate their understanding effectively.
4. **Build Confidence**
   Speaking in front of peers helps students develop self-assurance in their ability to articulate ideas fluently and expressively.

Why Use Oral Book Summaries?

1. **Reinforces Comprehension**
   Summarizing ensures students have a deep understanding of the text, as they must identify and articulate the most important points.
2. **Promotes Fluency Practice**
   Presenting summaries aloud helps students practice reading fluently and speaking with confidence.
3. **Encourages Expression**
   Oral presentations allow students to experiment with tone, pacing, and volume, enhancing their prosody.
4. **Builds Critical Thinking Skills**
   Choosing which details to include in a summary teaches students to evaluate and prioritize information.

How to Implement Oral Book Summaries

1. **Choose an Appropriate Book**
   Assign books that match students' reading levels and align with their interests. Encourage a variety of genres to expose students to diverse text structures.

   Example: For younger readers, use *Charlotte's Web* or *Frog and Toad Are Friends.* For older readers, consider *Holes* or *Number the Stars.*

2. **Guide Students in Creating Summaries**
   Teach students how to identify key elements of a summary, such as:
   - The main characters
   - The setting
   - The central conflict or problem
   - Key events
   - The resolution
3. **Provide a Template or Framework**
   Use sentence starters or graphic organizers to help students structure their summaries.
   Example Framework:
   - "The story is about ___."
   - "The main character, ___, faces ___."
   - "In the end, ___."
4. **Practice Fluency**
   Have students rehearse their summaries, focusing on clear articulation, proper pacing, and expressive delivery.

5. **Present to an Audience**
   Allow students to share their summaries with the class, in small groups, or even in pairs. Encourage active listening and positive feedback from peers.

Example Activity: Oral Book Summary

Step 1: Assign a book such as *Charlotte's Web.* After reading, ask students to create a summary.

Example Summary:

- "*Charlotte's Web* is about a pig named Wilbur who is saved from being slaughtered by his spider friend, Charlotte. She writes words in her web to make him famous. In the end, Wilbur lives, and Charlotte has baby spiders."

Step 2: Students practice delivering the summary aloud, using expressive tone and pacing.

Step 3: Have students present their summaries to the class, emphasizing clarity, confidence, and expression.

Variations of Oral Book Summaries

1. **Partner Summaries**
   Pair students to share their summaries with a partner before presenting to the class. This allows for practice and peer feedback.
2. **Creative Summaries**
   Encourage students to present their summaries creatively, such as acting out key scenes, creating a poster, or using props.
3. **Group Book Talks**
   Assign small groups the same book and have them collaborate on a group summary to present together.
4. **Digital Summaries**
   Allow students to record their summaries as audio or video presentations, which they can share with peers or parents.

Supporting Diverse Learners

1. **Struggling Readers**
   Use shorter, simpler texts and provide extra support in identifying key elements of the story. Allow more rehearsal time for oral delivery.

2. **Advanced Readers**
   Challenge advanced students to analyze deeper themes or compare the book to another text in their summary.
3. **English Language Learners (ELLs)**
   Provide sentence starters, visual aids, or vocabulary lists to support comprehension and oral expression.

Benefits Beyond Fluency

Oral book summaries strengthen a range of literacy skills, including:

- **Comprehension:** Summarizing ensures a deeper understanding of the text.
- **Vocabulary Development:** Students use and reinforce key words and phrases from the book.
- **Oral Communication:** Presenting summaries builds public speaking skills, preparing students for future academic and professional settings.

Troubleshooting Common Challenges

1. **What if students are nervous about speaking?**
   - Start with smaller audiences, such as presenting to a partner or small group, before moving to whole-class presentations.
2. **What if students struggle to identify key details?**
   - Provide guided questions or a summary template to help them focus on the most important parts of the story.
3. **What if students lose interest?**
   - Allow students to choose books that excite them, and incorporate creative presentation options to keep the activity engaging.

Incorporating Oral Book Summaries Into Daily Routines

- **Weekly Book Talks:** Set aside time each week for students to share their summaries.
- **Small-Group Discussions:** Use summaries as a starting point for deeper conversations about the book.
- **Morning Meetings:** Begin the day with a quick oral summary from one student.

Lesson Plan 1: Introduction to Oral Book Summaries

Grade Level: 3rd-5th Grade
Objective: Students will create and deliver a concise oral book summary, focusing on comprehension, fluency, and expression.

Materials Needed:

- Short books or excerpts (e.g., *Charlotte's Web*, *Frog and Toad Are Friends*)
- Summary framework handout (e.g., graphic organizer with prompts like "The story is about ___")
- Example summary written on the board
- Timer/stopwatch

Time Required: 40 minutes

Opening Script:
"Have you ever told someone about a great book you read? Today, we're going to practice doing just that by creating oral book summaries. You'll share the main ideas of your book in your own words, using expression and confidence to make it exciting for your audience!"

Define New Concepts (Script):

- **Oral Book Summary:** *"This is when you tell someone about a book you've read, explaining the main events, characters, and the ending in your own words."*
- **Fluency in Speaking:** *"This means speaking smoothly, with expression, and at a pace that's easy to understand."*

Activity Directions:

1. **Model the Process:**
    - Read an example summary aloud: *"Charlotte's Web is about a pig named Wilbur and his spider friend, Charlotte. Charlotte saves Wilbur by writing words in her web to make him famous. In the end, Wilbur lives, and Charlotte's baby spiders continue her legacy."*
    - Highlight how the summary includes the main character, conflict, key events, and resolution.

2. **Guided Practice:**
    - Distribute the summary framework handout.
    - Guide students through filling it out based on the book they've read.
    - Encourage them to write brief, clear sentences.
3. **Independent Practice:**
    - Students use their framework to practice saying their summary aloud in pairs, focusing on fluency and expression.
4. **Reflection:**
    - Discuss what made their summaries clear and engaging.

Assessment:

- Observe students' summaries for inclusion of key details.
- Note their fluency, pacing, and expression during practice.

Intervention:

- Provide struggling students with sentence starters or a sample summary to adapt.

Enrichment/Extension:

- Advanced students can add a personal opinion or connection to their summary, explaining why they recommend the book.

Lesson Plan 2: Partner Practice with Feedback

Grade Level: 4th-6th Grade
Objective: Students will practice delivering oral book summaries with a partner and provide constructive feedback.

Materials Needed:

- Books students have read (or short assigned texts)
- Peer feedback checklist (e.g., "Did they include the main character?" "Was their delivery clear and expressive?")
- Timer/stopwatch

Time Required: 45 minutes

Opening Script:
"Today, you'll work with a partner to practice sharing your book summary. You'll take turns presenting and giving each other feedback to make your summaries even better. It's teamwork for great storytelling!"

Define New Concepts (Script):

- **Feedback:** *"This means giving helpful suggestions about what your partner did well and how they can improve."*
- **Active Listening:** *"When you're the listener, focus on your partner's summary so you can give useful feedback."*

Activity Directions:

1. **Explain Partner Roles:**
   - One partner presents their summary while the other listens and completes the feedback checklist.
   - Switch roles after each presentation.
2. **Partner Practice:**
   - Set a timer for 2-3 minutes for each presentation.
   - After each summary, the listener shares one positive comment and one suggestion for improvement.

3. **Group Reflection:**
   - Discuss as a class: *"What made the best summaries stand out? How did feedback help?"*

Assessment:

- Collect feedback checklists to evaluate comprehension and delivery.
- Observe students' use of feedback to improve their summaries.

Intervention:

- Pair struggling readers with supportive peers. Provide additional time or practice for students who need it.

Enrichment/Extension:

- Advanced students can include a creative element in their presentation, such as acting out a scene or using visuals.

Lesson Plan 3: Group Book Talks with Creative Summaries

Grade Level: 5th-7th Grade
Objective: Students will collaborate on group summaries and creatively present their books to the class.

Materials Needed:

- Books assigned to groups
- Large paper or digital tools for creating visuals
- Props or costumes for creative presentations (optional)

Time Required: 1 hour

Opening Script:
"Today, you'll work in groups to create and present a summary of a book you've read. You can get creative—use visuals, act out a scene, or even make a poster. Your goal is to summarize the book in a way that makes your audience want to read it too!"

Define New Concepts (Script):

- **Group Summary:** *"This is when you work together to combine everyone's ideas into one clear summary of the book."*
- **Creative Presentation:** *"This means using tools like pictures, props, or acting to make your summary fun and engaging."*

Activity Directions:

1. **Group Work:**
   - Assign each group a book to summarize.
   - Groups use the summary framework to decide on the main points.
2. **Plan a Creative Presentation:**
   - Groups choose how to present their summary (e.g., acting, poster, or storytelling with props).
   - Rehearse the presentation as a team.
3. **Present to the Class:**
   - Each group presents their summary in 3-5 minutes.

- Encourage active listening by asking the audience to share one thing they learned from each group.

Assessment:

- Evaluate group presentations for clarity, fluency, and creativity.
- Observe collaboration and audience engagement.

Intervention:

- Assign simpler books or pair groups with a teacher assistant for support.

Enrichment/Extension:

- Advanced groups can compare their book to another story or theme in their presentation.

These lesson plans integrate comprehension, fluency, and creative expression, fostering both literacy and public speaking skills.

Conclusion

Oral book summaries are a powerful way to integrate fluency practice with comprehension and communication skills. By reading a book, summarizing its key points, and presenting the summary aloud, students deepen their understanding of the text while building confidence as fluent, expressive readers.

Whether summarizing *Charlotte's Web* or a favorite graphic novel, this strategy ensures students are not only reading but also thinking, speaking, and connecting. With each presentation, they grow as confident, articulate readers, ready to let their fluency flow in both reading and speaking.

Chapter 15

Mastering Rhythm and Expression: Poetry Practice

Poetry is a natural ally of fluency instruction. With its emphasis on rhythm, rhyme, and expression, poetry provides an engaging way for students to practice pacing, phrasing, and prosody (reading with expression). Its compact format and predictable patterns make it accessible to all readers, while its emotional depth and creativity inspire engagement and joy in reading.

Grounded in the science of reading, poetry practice supports fluency development by strengthening oral language skills, building automaticity, and encouraging expressive delivery. This chapter explores how poetry can be used as a tool for fluency, along with strategies to incorporate it effectively into your classroom.

Why Use Poetry for Fluency?

1. **Focuses on Rhythm and Pacing**
   Poetry's natural cadence helps students internalize the rhythm of language, improving their pacing and phrasing.
2. **Encourages Expression**
   Poems often evoke strong emotions or vivid imagery, inspiring students to experiment with tone, pitch, and volume in their oral reading.
3. **Supports Vocabulary Development**
   Poetry introduces rich and descriptive language, helping students expand their vocabulary in meaningful contexts.
4. **Engages Readers**
   The brevity and creativity of poems make them appealing and manageable for students, even those who may struggle with longer texts.

The Science Behind Poetry Practice

Fluency is more than reading quickly—it's about reading with accuracy, automaticity, and expression while understanding the text. Poetry practice aligns with the science of reading by:

1. **Reinforcing Phonological Awareness**
   The rhymes and rhythms in poetry strengthen students' ability to hear and manipulate sounds within words.
2. **Promoting Prosody**
   Poems encourage students to match their tone and expression to the mood and meaning of the text.
3. **Building Automaticity**
   Repeated readings of short, predictable poems help students recognize high-frequency words and common patterns more quickly.

How to Implement Poetry Practice

1. **Select a Poem**
   Choose poems that are age-appropriate, engaging, and aligned with students' fluency goals. Rhyming poems, nursery rhymes, and free verse all provide excellent opportunities for practice.
   Example Poem: *Twinkle, Twinkle, Little Star*
2. **Model Fluent Reading**
   Begin by reading the poem aloud, demonstrating proper pacing, rhythm, and expression. Discuss how you used your voice to bring the poem to life.
3. **Choral Reading**
   Have the class read the poem aloud together, focusing on maintaining a consistent rhythm and pace.
4. **Echo Reading**
   Read one line at a time and have students repeat it, mimicking your tone, expression, and rhythm.
5. **Independent Practice**
   Allow students to practice reading the poem individually or with a partner. Encourage them to experiment with expression and phrasing.
6. **Performance**
   Give students the opportunity to perform the poem for their peers, emphasizing fluency, expression, and confidence.

Example Activity: Poetry Practice with *Twinkle, Twinkle, Little Star*

Step 1: Model the poem by reading it aloud with rhythm and expression:

Twinkle, twinkle, little star,
How I wonder what you are!

Step 2: Lead the class in choral reading, ensuring everyone stays in rhythm.

Step 3: Have students practice in pairs, taking turns reading the poem aloud to each other.

Step 4: Encourage students to perform the poem individually or as a group, using expressive voices to convey the mood.

Variations of Poetry Practice

1. **Partner Poetry**
   Pair students to read poems aloud together, alternating lines or stanzas.
2. **Poetry Centers**
   Set up a fluency station with printed poems and whisper phones for students to practice reading aloud.
3. **Creative Expression**
   Allow students to add gestures, illustrations, or props to their poetry performance to enhance expression and engagement.
4. **Thematic Poetry**
   Choose poems that align with seasonal events or classroom themes. For example, use *Five Little Pumpkins* in October or *Auld Lang Syne* around New Year's.

Supporting Diverse Learners

1. **Struggling Readers**
   Use shorter, simpler poems with predictable rhymes and patterns. Provide extra modeling and guided practice.
2. **Advanced Readers**
   Challenge advanced students with more complex poetry that includes figurative language and varied structures.
3. **English Language Learners (ELLs)**
   Focus on poems with repetitive language and clear visuals. Discuss unfamiliar vocabulary before reading.

Benefits Beyond Fluency

Poetry practice not only develops fluency but also supports:

- **Comprehension:** Analyzing the meaning and mood of a poem deepens students' understanding of text.
- **Oral Communication:** Performing poetry builds confidence and public speaking skills.
- **Creativity:** Engaging with poetry encourages students to think imaginatively and expressively.

Troubleshooting Common Challenges

1. **What if students struggle with rhythm?**
    - Clap or tap out the rhythm of the poem before reading it aloud.
2. **What if students are shy about performing?**
    - Begin with group performances to build confidence, then move to smaller groups or individual recitations.
3. **What if students lose interest?**
    - Incorporate student choice by letting them select poems that resonate with their interests or emotions.

Incorporating Poetry Practice into Your Routine

- **Morning Warm-Up:** Start the day with a quick choral reading of a poem.
- **Fluency Centers:** Include poetry books or printed poems as part of a fluency-focused station.
- **Weekly Performances:** Dedicate a day each week for students to share and perform their favorite poems.

Lesson Plan 1: Introduction to Poetry Practice

Grade Level: 1st-3rd Grade
Objective: Students will practice fluency through rhythm, pacing, and expression by reading and performing a simple poem.

Materials Needed:

- Printed copies of *Twinkle, Twinkle, Little Star*
- Chart or whiteboard to display the poem
- Rhythm instruments (e.g., tambourine, clapping hands)

Time Required: 30 minutes

Opening Script:
"Have you ever noticed how some poems and songs have a rhythm that makes you want to clap along? Today, we're going to practice reading a poem with rhythm and expression. By the end, you'll be able to read it fluently, just like a performer!"

Define New Concepts (Script):

- **Fluency:** *"Fluency means reading smoothly and with expression, like you're telling a story to someone."*
- **Rhythm:** *"Rhythm is the beat or pattern in the poem that makes it flow."*

Activity Directions:

1. **Model Fluent Reading:**
   - Read *Twinkle, Twinkle, Little Star* aloud, emphasizing rhythm and expression.
   - Clap or tap the rhythm as you read.
2. **Choral Reading:**
   - Have the class read the poem aloud together, following your rhythm.
   - Encourage them to match your tone and pacing.
3. **Independent Practice:**
   - Students practice reading the poem in pairs, alternating lines.
   - Provide feedback on pacing and expression.
4. **Performance:**

- Invite volunteers to perform the poem for the class.
- Use rhythm instruments or clapping to enhance the presentation.

Assessment:

- Observe students' rhythm, pacing, and expression during choral and paired reading.
- Provide verbal feedback to individuals and pairs.

Intervention:

- Pair struggling readers with a stronger partner or practice one-on-one with the teacher.
- Use simpler poems or focus on one line at a time.

Enrichment/Extension:

- Advanced students can create their own short rhyming couplets to share with the class.

Lesson Plan 2: Partner Poetry Practice with Gestures

Grade Level: 2nd-4th Grade
Objective: Students will improve fluency and expression by incorporating gestures into their poetry reading.

Materials Needed:

- Printed copies of a simple poem (e.g., *Five Little Pumpkins*)
- List of suggested gestures for key lines (e.g., raising hands for "sat on a gate")

Time Required: 40 minutes

Opening Script:
"Have you ever seen someone act out a poem? Today, we'll bring a poem to life by adding gestures and expression to our reading. You'll work with a partner to practice fluency while making the poem fun and engaging!"

Define New Concepts (Script):

- **Gestures:** *"Gestures are movements that match the words you're saying. They help make the poem more exciting for your audience."*
- **Expression:** *"Expression means using your voice and body to show how the poem feels—happy, excited, or spooky!"*

Activity Directions:

1. **Model with Gestures:**
   - Read *Five Little Pumpkins* aloud while demonstrating gestures.
   - Example: Raise hands for "sat on a gate" and pretend to shiver for "the wind blew out the light."
2. **Partner Practice:**
   - Students work in pairs to rehearse the poem, deciding on gestures for each line.
   - Encourage them to practice fluency and expression.
3. **Group Reflection:**
   - Pairs perform their poem for another pair or small group.
   - Peers provide positive feedback on fluency and gestures.

Assessment:

- Observe students' fluency and creativity in using gestures.
- Use a checklist to track their ability to match gestures to the text.

Intervention:

- Offer pre-selected gestures for struggling readers to use.
- Focus on one stanza at a time for those needing additional support.

Enrichment/Extension:

- Advanced pairs can create a short skit or tableau to accompany their poem.

Lesson Plan 3: Thematic Poetry Performance

Grade Level: 3rd-5th Grade
Objective: Students will practice fluency by reading a themed poem aloud with rhythm, expression, and creativity.

Materials Needed:

- Thematic poems (e.g., *Auld Lang Syne* for New Year's or *In Flanders Fields* for Veterans Day)
- Props or visuals related to the theme
- Recording device (optional)

Time Required: 50 minutes

Opening Script:
"Poems often connect to special themes, like holidays or seasons. Today, you'll read a themed poem aloud and bring it to life with your voice and creativity. Let's explore how poetry can make a theme even more meaningful!"

Define New Concepts (Script):

- **Theme:** *"The theme is the main idea or feeling of a poem, like celebration or remembrance."*
- **Performance:** *"A performance means reading with rhythm, expression, and confidence while sharing the theme of the poem."*

Activity Directions:

1. **Discuss the Theme:**
   - Introduce the poem and discuss its theme and tone.
   - Example: "*Auld Lang Syne* is about remembering and celebrating the past."
2. **Small Group Practice:**
   - Divide students into small groups to rehearse reading the poem.
   - Encourage them to add creative elements, such as props or group gestures.
3. **Performance:**

   - Groups present their poems to the class, focusing on rhythm, expression, and creativity.
   - Optionally, record performances to review and reflect.
4. **Reflection:**
   - Discuss how each group's performance brought the theme to life.

Assessment:

- Use a rubric to evaluate fluency, expression, and creativity in performances.

Intervention:

- Provide simpler thematic poems for struggling readers.
- Offer additional practice and one-on-one support.

Enrichment/Extension:

- Advanced groups can write their own thematic poem to perform.

These lesson plans leverage the natural rhythm and emotional depth of poetry to build fluency while fostering creativity, comprehension, and engagement.

Conclusion

Poetry practice is a versatile and engaging way to develop reading fluency while nurturing creativity and expression. Whether students are exploring the rhythmic simplicity of *Twinkle, Twinkle, Little Star* or diving into the deeper meanings of a classic poem, they gain confidence in their ability to read with clarity, emotion, and understanding.

By incorporating poetry into your fluency instruction, you not only enhance students' reading skills but also foster a lifelong appreciation for the beauty and power of language. With each verse they master, their fluency flows more naturally, bringing the rhythm of reading to life.

Chapter 16

Strength in Numbers: Small-Group Interventions

Small-group interventions are a powerful way to provide focused fluency instruction tailored to the needs of struggling readers. These sessions create a supportive and structured environment where students can practice decoding, word recognition, and fluent reading with personalized guidance. By working in small groups, teachers can address specific challenges, monitor progress closely, and give students the tools they need to succeed.

Rooted in the science of reading, small-group interventions emphasize the systematic development of decoding skills and fluency. This chapter explores how small groups can be used effectively, strategies for implementation, and how they help students build confidence and competence as readers.

Why Use Small-Group Interventions?

The science of reading highlights the importance of targeted, explicit instruction in developing fluency, especially for struggling readers. Small-group interventions are effective because they:

1. **Provide Individualized Support**
   Teachers can focus on each student's unique needs, offering immediate feedback and guidance.
2. **Reinforce Decoding Skills**
   Small groups allow for intensive practice with phonics patterns and decoding strategies.
3. **Create a Safe Space**
   Students may feel more comfortable taking risks and making mistakes in a smaller, supportive group.
4. **Build Fluency Gradually**
   By practicing with decodable texts and manageable passages, students develop fluency one step at a time.

The Role of Small-Group Interventions in Fluency

Fluency is built on a foundation of decoding accuracy and automaticity. Small-group interventions address these elements by:

- **Targeting Specific Skills:** Focused sessions allow teachers to address challenges such as decoding multisyllabic words or improving pacing.
- **Providing Repetition:** Repeated practice with targeted texts helps reinforce fluency skills.
- **Promoting Confidence:** Success in a small group translates to greater self-assurance when reading independently or in larger settings.

How to Implement Small-Group Interventions

1. **Assess and Group Students**
   Use assessment data to group students based on their specific needs, such as decoding CVC words, mastering digraphs, or reading multisyllabic words fluently.
2. **Select Decodable Texts**
   Choose passages that align with the phonics skills students have mastered or are currently learning.
   Example Passage:
   - *The big red fox ran up the hill to the pond.*
3. **Break Down Words**
   Focus on challenging words by teaching students to break them into syllables or phonetic chunks.
   Example Word:
   - *Elephant*: Break it into *el-e-phant* and practice each syllable before blending them.
4. **Practice Fluency with Repetition**
   Have students read the passage multiple times, each time focusing on a specific goal, such as accuracy, speed, or expression.
5. **Incorporate Echo and Choral Reading**
   Model fluent reading of the passage, then have students echo or read it together as a group.
6. **Provide Immediate Feedback**
   Offer constructive feedback to help students correct errors, refine their pacing, and improve expression.

Example Activity: Small-Group Fluency Session

Focus: Decoding and reading fluency with multisyllabic words.

Step 1: Begin with a quick warm-up of familiar phonics patterns or high-frequency words.

- Example Words: *sun, cat, jump*

Step 2: Introduce a decodable passage, such as:

- *An elephant sat on a big black mat. It was so heavy that the mat broke!*

Step 3: Model fluent reading of the passage, emphasizing proper pacing and expression.

Step 4: Break down challenging words like *elephant* into syllables, helping students decode them step by step.

Step 5: Have students read the passage aloud individually or in pairs, providing feedback on their fluency.

Step 6: End with a group choral reading to build confidence and reinforce fluency.

Variations of Small-Group Interventions

1. **Partner Practice**
   Pair students within the group to read passages aloud to each other, providing peer feedback and support.
2. **Fluency Games**
   Incorporate games like *Word Race* (timing how quickly students can decode a list of words) or *Fluency Bingo* (reading phrases to cover bingo squares).
3. **Syllable Sorting**
   Use word cards with multisyllabic words and have students sort them by syllable patterns (e.g., *open, closed, VCe*).
4. **Guided Writing**
   After reading a passage, have students write their own sentences or stories using the same phonics patterns or challenging words.

Supporting Diverse Learners

1. **Struggling Readers**
   Focus on shorter passages and simpler words. Provide ample modeling and repetition to build confidence.
2. **Advanced Readers**
   Challenge students with longer texts, complex sentence structures, or fluency goals like reading with dramatic expression.
3. **English Language Learners (ELLs)**
   Incorporate visual aids, gestures, or translations to support comprehension and fluency.

Monitoring Progress in Small Groups

1. **Fluency Assessments**
   Use tools like timed readings or words-per-minute (WPM) tracking to measure growth over time.
2. **Observation Checklists**
   Track student progress in decoding, accuracy, pacing, and expression during group sessions.
3. **Student Reflection**
   Encourage students to reflect on their progress by sharing what they've learned or setting goals for future sessions.

Benefits Beyond Fluency

Small-group interventions help students develop essential skills, including:

- **Comprehension:** Decoding accurately leads to better understanding of text.
- **Confidence:** Success in a small group empowers students to read aloud in larger settings.
- **Collaboration:** Group activities foster teamwork and peer support.

Troubleshooting Common Challenges

1. **What if students struggle with multisyllabic words?**
   - Break the words into smaller chunks and provide repeated practice with similar patterns.
2. **What if students lose focus?**
   - Keep sessions short and engaging. Use hands-on activities or games to maintain interest.

3. **What if students feel discouraged?**
    - Celebrate small victories and provide constant positive reinforcement to build their confidence.

Incorporating Small-Group Interventions Into Your Routine

- **Daily Practice:** Dedicate 15–20 minutes daily for small-group fluency work.
- **Station Rotations:** Include small-group instruction as part of a literacy center rotation.
- **Intervention Blocks:** Use targeted small groups during intervention or enrichment periods.

Lesson Plan 1: Introduction to Small-Group Interventions

Grade Level: 1st-3rd Grade
Objective: Students will practice decoding and fluency with targeted support in a small group, focusing on multisyllabic words.

Materials Needed:

- Word cards with multisyllabic words (e.g., elephant, fantastic)
- Decodable passages (e.g., *An elephant sat on a big black mat.*)
- Whiteboard or chart for modeling
- Timer/stopwatch

Time Required: 25 minutes

Opening Script:
"Have you ever seen a really long word and wondered how to read it? Today, we'll work together in a small group to break down tricky words into smaller parts and practice reading a fun passage fluently. With teamwork, we'll make big words easy!"

Define New Concepts (Script):

- **Decoding:** *"This means breaking words into smaller parts, or syllables, so we can read them more easily."*
- **Fluency:** *"Fluency is reading smoothly and with expression, like we're telling a story."*

Activity Directions:

1. **Warm-Up:**
   - Show word cards with multisyllabic words.
   - Model breaking a word into syllables (e.g., el-e-phant).
   - Have students repeat after you.
2. **Guided Reading:**
   - Introduce a short decodable passage: *An elephant sat on a big black mat. It was so heavy that the mat broke!*
   - Model fluent reading, then have students read it together (choral reading).
3. **Individual Practice:**

  - Students take turns reading the passage aloud, focusing on accuracy and expression.
  - Provide feedback on pacing and decoding.
4. **Group Reflection:**
    - Discuss what strategies helped them read the passage smoothly.

Assessment:

- Observe students' decoding and fluency during individual practice.
- Track accuracy and expression using a checklist.

Intervention:

- For struggling readers, provide extra modeling and focus on simpler words.
- Use a smaller portion of the passage for repeated practice.

Enrichment/Extension:

- Advanced students can create their own sentences using the words practiced.

Lesson Plan 2: Partner Practice with Fluency Games

Grade Level: 2nd-4th Grade
Objective: Students will develop fluency through partner reading and engaging fluency games in a small group setting.

Materials Needed:

- Decodable passages or short stories
- Word Race game cards with challenging words
- Fluency Bingo boards with phrases or sentences

Time Required: 30 minutes

Opening Script:
"Let's turn reading into a game! Today, we'll practice reading fluently with a partner, and then we'll play some fun games to help us build speed, accuracy, and confidence. Ready to race to fluency?"

Define New Concepts (Script):

- **Fluency Games:** *"These are activities that help us read faster and better while having fun. They make practice exciting!"*

Activity Directions:

1. **Partner Reading:**
   - Pair students and provide a short decodable passage.
   - Partners take turns reading aloud and giving feedback (e.g., *"Try to pause at the comma here."*).
2. **Fluency Game 1: Word Race:**
   - Lay out word cards. Set a timer for one minute.
   - Partners take turns reading as many words as they can in the time limit. Track scores to encourage improvement.
3. **Fluency Game 2: Bingo:**
   - Provide Bingo boards with phrases or sentences.

   - Students read the phrases aloud to mark their boards. The first to complete a row wins.
4. **Group Reflection:**
   - Share what strategies helped them improve during the games.

Assessment:

- Track progress during Word Race by noting words read correctly per minute.
- Observe fluency and expression during partner reading.

Intervention:

- Provide simpler word cards and phrases for students who need extra support.

Enrichment/Extension:

- Challenge advanced students to create their own word cards or Bingo boards for peers.

Lesson Plan 3: Choral Reading and Syllable Sorting

Grade Level: 3rd-5th Grade
Objective: Students will practice fluency through choral reading and reinforce decoding skills with a hands-on syllable-sorting activity.

Materials Needed:

- Decodable passages with multisyllabic words
- Word cards with multisyllabic words (e.g., fantastic, wonderful, impossible)
- Syllable sorting mats (labeled: Open, Closed, VCe)

Time Required: 40 minutes

Opening Script:
"Reading big words can feel like solving a puzzle. Today, we'll practice reading together as a group, and then we'll break down tricky words to figure out their syllables. By the end, you'll be a word expert!"

Define New Concepts (Script):

- **Syllables:** *"Syllables are the beats in a word. For example, fan-tas-tic has three syllables."*
- **Choral Reading:** *"This means reading together as a group, matching our voices and pace."*

Activity Directions:

1. **Choral Reading:**
   - Introduce a passage (e.g., *The fantastic elephant jumped over the fence*).
   - Read aloud together, emphasizing pacing and rhythm.
2. **Syllable Sorting Activity:**
   - Distribute word cards.
   - Model how to break a word into syllables (e.g., fan-tas-tic).
   - Have students sort words onto syllable mats.
3. **Fluency Practice:**
   - Students read the sorted words aloud, focusing on smooth blending of syllables.

4. **Reflection:**
   - Discuss how breaking words into syllables helped with reading fluency.

Assessment:

- Observe students' ability to decode and sort words accurately.
- Listen for fluency improvements during choral reading.

Intervention:

- Provide visual aids or sentence frames for struggling readers.
- Use simpler, one-syllable words as a warm-up.

Enrichment/Extension:

- Advanced students can write their own multisyllabic words to challenge the group.

These plans use small-group settings to support fluency development through targeted instruction, engaging activities, and differentiated strategies, ensuring all students experience success.

Conclusion

Small-group interventions are a cornerstone of effective fluency instruction, providing the individualized attention and targeted practice students need to grow as readers. By focusing on decoding and fluency in a supportive setting, teachers can empower struggling readers to master challenging words, build confidence, and develop the skills necessary for independent reading.

Whether students are decoding words like *elephant* or reading sentences about *big black mats*, small-group interventions ensure every learner has the tools and support to let their fluency flow.

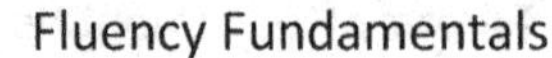

Chapter 17

Building Independence: Self-Monitoring Strategies

Self-monitoring is a critical component of fluency that empowers students to recognize and correct their own reading errors. By teaching students to pause, reflect, and reread when they encounter a mistake, you help them develop independence, accuracy, and confidence in their reading abilities. Self-monitoring is not just about catching errors—it's about fostering a growth mindset where students actively engage with the text to ensure comprehension and fluency.

Grounded in the science of reading, self-monitoring strategies align with the principles of metacognition, or thinking about one's own thinking. These strategies help students develop a deeper awareness of their reading processes, enabling them to adjust and improve in real time.

The Science Behind Self-Monitoring

Fluency involves not only reading words accurately and expressively but also recognizing when something doesn't sound right. Self-monitoring builds this skill by:

1. **Encouraging Active Engagement**
   Students learn to listen to themselves as they read, increasing their awareness of errors and fluency.
2. **Reinforcing Decoding Skills**
   Correcting errors often requires students to return to the word, decode it accurately, and apply phonics rules.
3. **Promoting Comprehension**
   When students reread for accuracy, they improve their understanding of the text by ensuring that the words and sentences make sense.
4. **Fostering Independence**
   Self-monitoring helps students take ownership of their learning, reducing reliance on teacher intervention.

Why Teach Self-Monitoring Strategies?

1. **Improves Accuracy**
   Students learn to catch and correct their mistakes, leading to more accurate reading.
2. **Builds Fluency**
   Rereading sentences after correcting errors helps students practice smoother, more expressive reading.
3. **Develops Confidence**
   Knowing how to identify and fix mistakes gives students the confidence to tackle challenging texts.
4. **Encourages Lifelong Skills**
   Self-monitoring extends beyond the classroom, preparing students to become independent, reflective readers.

How to Teach Self-Monitoring Strategies

1. **Model Self-Monitoring**
   Read a passage aloud and intentionally make a mistake. Pause and say, "Wait, that didn't sound right. Let me try again." Correct the error and reread the sentence fluently.

   Example:

   - Initial Reading: *"The cap sat on the mat."*
   - Self-Correction: "Wait, I said 'cap,' but that doesn't make sense. The word is 'cat.' Let me reread: 'The cat sat on the mat.'"
2. **Teach Students to Pause and Reread**
   Emphasize the importance of stopping when something doesn't sound right and rereading the sentence for accuracy.
3. **Use Visual Cues**
   Provide bookmarks or anchor charts with prompts like:
   - "Does that make sense?"
   - "Does that sound right?"
   - "Does that look right?"
4. **Practice in Small Steps**
   Start with short sentences or phrases. Gradually increase the length and complexity of the text as students become more confident.
5. **Encourage Peer Feedback**
   Pair students to listen to each other read. Encourage them to help their partner identify and correct errors.

Example Activity: Self-Monitoring in Action

Step 1: Provide a short decodable passage, such as:

- *The big red dog ran to the park.*

Step 2: Have a student read the passage aloud. If they misread a word (e.g., *park* as *part*), gently guide them to self-correct:

- Teacher: "Does 'The big red dog ran to the part' make sense?"
- Student: "No, it doesn't."
- Teacher: "What do you think the word is? Try again."

Step 3: Once the student identifies the correct word, have them reread the entire sentence fluently.

Variations of Self-Monitoring Activities

1. **Error Hunt**
   Provide a passage with intentional errors and have students identify and correct them.
2. **Rereading for Fluency**
   After self-correcting, students practice rereading the passage multiple times to improve fluency and confidence.
3. **Partner Practice**
   Pair students to take turns reading and monitoring. One student reads aloud while the other listens and provides feedback on errors.
4. **Reflection Journals**
   Have students keep a journal where they record the errors they catch and reflect on how they fixed them.

Supporting Diverse Learners

1. **Struggling Readers**
   Provide extra scaffolding, such as word banks or guided practice, to help them identify and correct errors.
2. **Advanced Readers**
   Challenge them with longer passages or more complex texts, focusing on self-monitoring for nuanced phrasing and expression.
3. **English Language Learners (ELLs)**
   Offer sentence frames or visuals to support comprehension and self-monitoring in a second language.

Benefits Beyond Fluency

Self-monitoring strategies enhance fluency while also supporting:

- **Comprehension:** Rereading sentences ensures students understand what they've read.
- **Critical Thinking:** Students learn to analyze their own reading for accuracy and meaning.
- **Independence:** Developing self-monitoring skills fosters lifelong reading habits.

Troubleshooting Common Challenges

1. **What if students don't notice their mistakes?**
   - Provide prompts like, "Does that sound right?" or "What would make sense here?"
2. **What if students feel frustrated?**
   - Emphasize progress over perfection and celebrate small successes to build confidence.
3. **What if students rely too much on the teacher?**
   - Gradually reduce support by encouraging peer feedback or independent practice.

Incorporating Self-Monitoring Strategies Into Daily Routines

- **Morning Reading Warm-Up:** Start the day with a short self-monitoring exercise, such as correcting a sentence together.
- **Small-Group Work:** Use guided reading sessions to practice self-monitoring with teacher support.
- **Independent Practice:** Encourage students to self-monitor during silent reading or homework assignments.

Lesson Plan 1: Introduction to Self-Monitoring Strategies

Grade Level: 2nd-4th Grade
Objective: Students will learn to recognize and correct reading errors using self-monitoring strategies.

Materials Needed:

- Simple decodable passages (e.g., *The cat sat on the mat.*)
- Visual aids (e.g., bookmarks or posters with self-monitoring prompts: *"Does that make sense?"*)
- Whiteboard or chart for modeling mistakes

Time Required: 30 minutes

Opening Script:
"Have you ever read something and thought, 'That doesn't sound right'? That's your brain noticing a mistake! Today, we'll learn how to listen carefully as we read and fix errors to make sure everything sounds and makes sense. This skill is called self-monitoring."

Define New Concepts (Script):

- **Self-Monitoring:** *"This means checking your own reading to make sure it sounds right, looks right, and makes sense."*
- **Rereading:** *"When you find a mistake, you go back, fix it, and read the sentence again so it flows smoothly."*

Activity Directions:

1. **Model Self-Monitoring:**
   - Write a sentence on the board: *The cat sat on the mat.*
   - Read it aloud, intentionally making a mistake: *"The cat sat on the man."*
   - Say: *"Wait, that doesn't make sense. Let me try again: 'The cat sat on the mat.' That sounds right!"*
2. **Guided Practice:**
   - Distribute passages with simple sentences.

  - Have students read aloud individually or in pairs. If they make an error, prompt them with: *"Does that make sense?"* or *"Try that word again."*
3. **Independent Practice:**
   - Students practice self-monitoring as they read a short passage silently.
   - They circle or underline words they correct and reread the sentence fluently.
4. **Reflection:**
   - Discuss how self-monitoring helps with accurate and smooth reading.

Assessment:

- Observe students during guided and independent practice, noting how often they self-correct.
- Review the words they identify and fix independently.

Intervention:

- Provide extra support for struggling readers by reading sentences aloud together and modeling corrections step-by-step.

Enrichment/Extension:

- Advanced students can monitor fluency in longer texts, focusing on phrasing and expression.

Lesson Plan 2: Error Hunt Activity

Grade Level: 3rd-5th Grade
Objective: Students will identify and correct intentional errors in a passage, practicing self-monitoring strategies.

Materials Needed:

- Passages with pre-made intentional errors (e.g., *The dog dug in the sad* instead of *sand*)
- Self-monitoring bookmarks with prompts
- Highlighters or colored pencils

Time Required: 35 minutes

Opening Script:
"Today, you're going on an error hunt! I've hidden mistakes in a story, and your job is to find and fix them. You'll use your self-monitoring skills to make sure every sentence sounds and makes sense."

Define New Concepts (Script):

- **Error Hunt:** *"This is when you carefully read a passage, looking for words or phrases that don't fit. When you find an error, you fix it and reread the sentence fluently."*

Activity Directions:

1. **Explain the Task:**
   - Provide an example sentence with an error: *The sun set in the west, and the sky turned blue.* Change *blue* to *red* to demonstrate.
   - Say: *"Blue doesn't make sense here. The sky turns red at sunset. Let's fix it and reread the sentence."*
2. **Guided Practice:**
   - Read the first two sentences of the passage aloud as a group, finding and fixing errors together.
3. **Independent Error Hunt:**
   - Students read the rest of the passage silently, highlighting errors and writing corrections.

   - Encourage them to use bookmarks for prompts like: *"Does that sound right?"*
4. **Partner Check:**
   - Students pair up to compare corrections and practice reading the passage fluently.

Assessment:

- Collect highlighted passages to evaluate accuracy in identifying and correcting errors.
- Observe partner readings for fluency improvements.

Intervention:

- Use simpler passages with fewer errors for struggling students. Provide additional modeling before independent practice.

Enrichment/Extension:

- Challenge advanced students to create their own error-filled passages for peers to solve.

Lesson Plan 3: Reflection Journals for Self-Monitoring

Grade Level: 4th-6th Grade
Objective: Students will reflect on their self-monitoring process, identifying and explaining errors they corrected.

Materials Needed:

- Decodable passages
- Self-monitoring journals or notebooks
- Sentence starters for reflection (e.g., *"I noticed that I misread the word ___ because ___. I fixed it by ___."*)

Time Required: 40 minutes

Opening Script:
"Today, you'll practice fixing your own mistakes as you read and write about how you did it. This will help you think about how self-monitoring works and how it helps you become a better reader."

Define New Concepts (Script):

- **Reflection Journals:** *"A place where you write about what you learned, the mistakes you fixed, and how you fixed them."*

Activity Directions:

1. **Reading with Reflection:**
   - Provide a passage.
   - Students read aloud, stopping to note any mistakes they make.
   - Encourage them to jot down corrections in their journal.
2. **Reflection Writing:**
   - Use sentence starters to guide students in writing about their process:
     "I noticed that I misread the word 'sand' as 'sad.' I fixed it by looking at the other words in the sentence."
3. **Sharing and Discussion:**

  - Students share one correction and how they fixed it with a small group or the class.

4. **Fluency Practice:**
   - Reread the corrected passage aloud for smoother delivery.

Assessment:

- Review journals for thoughtful reflection on errors and strategies used.
- Listen to rereadings for improved fluency.

Intervention:

- Pair struggling students with a peer or teacher to discuss and write about corrections.

Enrichment/Extension:

- Advanced students can analyze why certain errors occurred and suggest strategies to avoid them in the future.

These lesson plans encourage students to build independence and confidence as readers by mastering self-monitoring strategies, fostering both fluency and a growth mindset.

Conclusion

Self-monitoring strategies are essential for developing fluent, independent readers. By teaching students to recognize and correct their own errors, you help them build accuracy, confidence, and comprehension skills that will serve them throughout their lives.

Whether they're rereading a simple sentence like *"The cat sat on the mat"* or tackling more complex texts, self-monitoring empowers students to take ownership of their learning. With these strategies in place, fluency flows naturally, turning mistakes into opportunities for growth.

Chapter 18

The Power of Technology: Integrating Digital Tools for Fluency

Technology offers an exciting and effective way to enhance fluency instruction, providing students with opportunities for independent practice, real-time feedback, and personalized growth. By incorporating apps, programs, and digital tools into fluency practice, teachers can meet the diverse needs of students while leveraging the benefits of immediate feedback and engagement.

Grounded in the science of reading, technology integration supports fluency development by combining repetition, feedback, and interactive learning. This chapter explores the role of technology in fluency instruction, practical strategies for implementation, and how it empowers students to take ownership of their learning.

The Science Behind Technology Integration

The science of reading emphasizes the importance of frequent, focused practice and timely feedback for developing fluency. Technology supports these principles by:

1. **Providing Real-Time Feedback**
   Digital tools can analyze students' reading for accuracy, pace, and expression, offering immediate insights that help them improve.
2. **Enabling Independent Practice**
   Apps and programs allow students to practice fluency at their own pace, freeing up teacher time for targeted instruction.
3. **Reinforcing Repetition**
   Technology encourages repeated practice of passages, which strengthens automaticity and confidence.
4. **Engaging Diverse Learners**
   Interactive features like gamification, audio playback, and visual aids make fluency practice engaging and accessible for all students.

Why Use Technology for Fluency?

1. **Personalized Feedback**
   Technology provides tailored feedback, helping students understand specific areas for improvement.
2. **Increased Motivation**
   Gamified elements, progress tracking, and rewards systems keep students motivated to practice fluency.
3. **Flexibility and Accessibility**
   Students can practice anytime, anywhere, making fluency development more consistent and convenient.
4. **Teacher Support**
   Apps and tools collect data on student performance, allowing teachers to monitor progress and adjust instruction accordingly.

How to Implement Technology for Fluency

1. **Select the Right Tools**
   Choose apps or programs that align with your instructional goals and provide features such as audio recording, feedback, and progress tracking.
   Examples of Fluency Tools:
   - Apps like *Raz-Kids* or *Fluency Tutor*
   - Programs with AI-powered feedback such as *Learning Ally* or *Read Naturally Live*
2. **Introduce the Tool to Students**
   Demonstrate how to use the app or program, including how to record passages, review feedback, and track progress.
3. **Create a Routine**
   Incorporate technology into daily or weekly routines, such as a fluency station during literacy centers or a homework assignment.
4. **Provide Guidance and Support**
   While students practice independently, monitor their progress and provide additional instruction when needed.
5. **Set Goals**
   Help students set specific fluency goals, such as improving words per minute (WPM) or enhancing expression, and use the technology to track their achievements.

Example Activity: Using Technology for Fluency

Step 1: Assign a passage on a reading app, such as:

- *The dog ran to the park and jumped over the bench.*

Step 2: Have students record themselves reading the passage aloud.

Step 3: The app provides feedback on their pace, accuracy, and expression, highlighting areas for improvement.

Step 4: Students reread the passage, applying the feedback, and record it again to measure their growth.

Step 5: Review their progress together, celebrating improvements and setting new goals.

Variations of Technology Integration

1. **Audio Playback**
   Use apps that allow students to listen to their recordings, helping them self-monitor for fluency and accuracy.
2. **Gamified Fluency Practice**
   Incorporate programs with game-like features, such as earning badges or points for completing reading challenges.
3. **Interactive E-Books**
   Provide access to digital books with built-in narration and fluency prompts.
4. **Peer Feedback**
   Pair students to listen to each other's recordings and provide constructive feedback using the app.

Supporting Diverse Learners

1. **Struggling Readers**
   Use tools with built-in scaffolds, such as word highlighting, audio support, or adjustable reading speeds.
2. **Advanced Readers**
   Challenge advanced readers with longer passages or more complex texts, focusing on nuanced expression and pacing.
3. **English Language Learners (ELLs)**
   Use apps that offer translation, pronunciation guides, or visuals to support comprehension and fluency.

Benefits Beyond Fluency

Technology integration supports fluency while also enhancing:

- **Comprehension:** Features like vocabulary support and text analysis deepen understanding.
- **Confidence:** Real-time feedback and progress tracking boost students' self-assurance in their reading abilities.
- **Digital Literacy:** Students develop skills in navigating technology, preparing them for future learning environments.

Troubleshooting Common Challenges

1. **What if students misuse the technology?**
    - Set clear expectations and monitor usage to ensure students stay focused on their fluency practice.
2. **What if students are overwhelmed by feedback?**
    - Help students interpret the feedback and focus on one area of improvement at a time.
3. **What if technology isn't available at home?**
    - Provide time during the school day for students to use the tools, such as in a fluency station or during intervention blocks.

Incorporating Technology Into Daily Routines

- **Fluency Centers:** Set up a station with tablets or computers for fluency practice using apps or programs.
- **Homework Assignments:** Assign passages for students to record and practice at home.
- **Progress Monitoring:** Use technology to collect data on fluency growth and inform instruction.

Lesson Plan 1: Introduction to Fluency Apps

Grade Level: 3rd-5th Grade
Objective: Students will learn to use a reading app to practice fluency, receive feedback, and track progress.

Materials Needed:

- Tablets or computers with a fluency app installed (e.g., Raz-Kids, Fluency Tutor)
- Headphones
- Short passages within the app

Time Required: 35 minutes

Opening Script:
"Have you ever wished you could hear yourself read or get instant help to improve? Today, we'll use a special app to practice reading fluently. It will let you record your voice, get feedback, and watch yourself improve over time!"

Define New Concepts (Script):

- **Fluency App:** *"A digital tool that helps you practice reading by listening to your voice and giving you feedback."*
- **Feedback:** *"Suggestions that help you read better, like noticing if you missed a word or read too fast."*

Activity Directions:

1. **Introduce the App:**
   - Demonstrate how to log in, select a passage, and record reading aloud.
   - Show how to review the feedback provided by the app (e.g., WPM, accuracy, and expression).
2. **Guided Practice:**
   - Assign each student a passage to read on the app.
   - Monitor students as they record themselves and review the feedback.
3. **Independent Practice:**
   - Students reread the passage, applying the app's feedback to improve fluency.

   - Record the second attempt and compare the results.
4. **Reflection:**
   - Discuss: *"What did you learn from the feedback? How did your second recording improve?"*

Assessment:

- Review app-generated reports for accuracy, WPM, and expression.
- Observe students during practice to assess engagement and effort.

Intervention:

- Pair struggling readers with a teacher or peer for extra guidance on using the app and interpreting feedback.

Enrichment/Extension:

- Advanced students can practice longer or more complex passages, focusing on nuanced expression.

Lesson Plan 2: Audio Playback and Self-Monitoring

Grade Level: 4th-6th Grade
Objective: Students will use audio playback to self-monitor their fluency and identify areas for improvement.

Materials Needed:

- Tablets or computers with recording functionality (built-in or app-based)
- Short passages for practice (printed and digital)
- Self-monitoring checklist (e.g., *Did I read smoothly? Did I pronounce all the words correctly?*)

Time Required: 40 minutes

Opening Script:
"Have you ever listened to yourself read? It's a great way to notice what you're doing well and what you can improve. Today, you'll record your reading, listen to it, and use a checklist to find ways to make it even better!"

Define New Concepts (Script):

- **Audio Playback:** *"Listening to your own voice after you read to check how you did."*
- **Self-Monitoring:** *"Paying attention to how you're reading and making changes to improve."*

Activity Directions:

1. **Model the Process:**
   - Record yourself reading a short passage and play it back for the class.
   - Complete the self-monitoring checklist as a group.
2. **Student Practice:**
   - Students record themselves reading their assigned passage.
   - Listen to the playback and use the checklist to identify strengths and areas for improvement.
3. **Re-Record and Reflect:**
   - Students reread the passage, focusing on the areas they want to improve.

  - Record a second attempt and compare it to the first.
4. **Group Discussion:**
  - Share: *"What did you notice about your reading? How did you improve?"*

Assessment:

- Collect self-monitoring checklists to evaluate students' ability to reflect on their reading.
- Listen to recordings to track fluency progress.

Intervention:

- Provide sentence starters or visual cues for struggling readers to help them complete the checklist.

Enrichment/Extension:

- Advanced students can analyze their pacing and expression in longer recordings, focusing on improving prosody.

Lesson Plan 3: Fluency Games with Technology

Grade Level: 2nd-4th Grade
Objective: Students will engage with gamified fluency tools to practice reading accuracy, speed, and expression.

Materials Needed:

- Tablets or computers with a gamified fluency app (e.g., Epic!, Read Naturally Live)
- Headphones
- Progress tracking sheet for rewards

Time Required: 30 minutes

Opening Script:
"Who's ready to play a reading game? Today, we'll use a special app that turns fluency practice into a fun challenge. You'll earn points and rewards as you improve your reading!"

Define New Concepts (Script):

- **Gamified Learning:** *"When a learning activity is set up like a game, with challenges and rewards to keep it fun."*
- **Fluency Goals:** *"Targets like reading faster or smoother that you try to reach while playing."*

Activity Directions:

1. **Explain the Game:**
   - Show how to log in and navigate the app.
   - Demonstrate how points or badges are earned by completing fluency tasks.
2. **Independent Practice:**
   - Students select a passage or challenge on the app and begin practicing.
   - Monitor their engagement and encourage them to set personal fluency goals (e.g., improve WPM by 5 words).
3. **Reflection and Rewards:**
   - After the session, review progress on the app and celebrate milestones (e.g., *"You earned 3 badges today!"*).

4. **Wrap-Up:**
    - Discuss how the app helped them practice fluency.

Assessment:

- Review app progress reports to evaluate gains in accuracy and speed.
- Note student engagement and goal-setting during practice.

Intervention:

- Assist students struggling with the app by providing hands-on guidance or simplifying their tasks.

Enrichment/Extension:

- Advanced students can create their own reading challenges or mentor peers in using the app effectively.

These plans integrate technology into fluency practice, leveraging digital tools to provide immediate feedback, foster self-monitoring, and motivate students through gamification and progress tracking.

Chapter 19

Charting Success: Fluency Graphing

Fluency graphing is a dynamic and highly effective strategy that motivates students by providing a visual representation of their reading progress over time. This process involves tracking key fluency metrics, such as Words Per Minute (WPM), and plotting them on a graph. By transforming fluency development into a measurable and goal-driven process, students are empowered to take ownership of their progress, celebrate their achievements, and stay motivated to improve further.

Rooted in the principles of the science of reading, fluency graphing promotes repeated practice, data-driven instruction, and the importance of setting achievable goals. This chapter provides a step-by-step guide to implementing fluency graphing, highlights its numerous benefits, and explores how it aligns with research-based best practices in fluency instruction.

The Science Behind Fluency Graphing

Fluency development relies on consistent, intentional practice and ongoing progress monitoring. Research from the science of reading emphasizes the importance of regular assessment and timely feedback, as they allow students to track their growth and pinpoint areas requiring improvement. Fluency graphing complements these principles in several ways:

1. **Encouraging Repeated Practice**
   Timed readings provide structured opportunities for students to reread texts, enhancing their automaticity, word recognition, and overall confidence.
2. **Highlighting Progress**
   Graphing fluency scores makes student growth tangible. A steadily rising line on a graph visually demonstrates improvement, motivating students to continue practicing.
3. **Setting Clear Goals**
   Fluency graphing helps students set realistic, measurable objectives for their progress, fostering a sense of achievement when milestones are reached.
4. **Promoting Self-Reflection**
   Through graphing, students gain insight into their performance, learn to analyze their strengths and challenges, and understand the consistent effort needed to improve their fluency skills.

Why Use Fluency Graphing?

Fluency graphing offers unique benefits for both students and educators:

1. **Motivates Students**
   Visualizing progress on a graph inspires students to take ownership of their learning. The act of seeing their success encourages persistence and builds intrinsic motivation.
2. **Builds Confidence**
   Celebrating small but meaningful gains boosts students' self-esteem and reinforces their belief in their reading abilities.
3. **Provides Insight for Teachers**
   Graphing gives teachers a clear overview of individual and class-wide progress, enabling them to identify trends and tailor instruction to meet students' needs.
4. **Encourages Goal Setting**
   Setting and achieving goals develops essential life skills, helping students learn the value of perseverance and planning.

How to Implement Fluency Graphing

Fluency graphing is straightforward to implement and can be seamlessly integrated into literacy instruction. Follow these steps to get started:

1. **Conduct a Timed Reading**
   Select a passage that matches the student's reading level. Set a timer for one minute and have the student read aloud. Count the number of words read correctly (WPM).
2. **Record the Score**
   Write down the student's WPM score from the timed reading session. Ensure that this is done accurately to track progress effectively.
3. **Create a Graph**
   Provide each student with a blank graph, clearly labeled with dates on the x-axis and WPM scores on the y-axis.
4. **Plot Progress**
   After each timed reading, guide the student to plot their score on the graph and connect the dots to create a visual record of their progress.
5. **Set Goals**
   Collaboratively set achievable, short-term goals, such as increasing WPM by 5 words in a week or improving reading expression.
6. **Celebrate Growth**
   Acknowledge and celebrate every improvement, no matter how small. Recognizing effort builds students' confidence and encourages continued practice.

Example Activity: Fluency Graphing

1. Select a simple passage, such as:
   "The cat ran up the hill. It saw a big red barn and stopped to look inside."
2. Conduct a one-minute timed reading and record the WPM score (e.g., 50 WPM).
3. Provide a blank graph to the student. Plot the score together:
   - Date: January 15 | WPM: 50
4. Repeat this activity weekly. Over time, the graph might show steady progress:
   - January 15: 50 WPM
   - January 22: 55 WPM
   - January 29: 60 WPM

Variations of Fluency Graphing

1. **Group Graphing**
   Create a class-wide graph to track collective progress. This fosters teamwork and a sense of shared achievement.
2. **Expression Graphs**
   Instead of WPM, focus on other fluency metrics like expression or accuracy. Use rubrics to score and graph these aspects.
3. **Digital Graphing Tools**
   Incorporate technology by using apps or software to create digital fluency graphs. These tools make progress tracking interactive and engaging.
4. **Themed Graphs**
   Add creativity by using seasonal or themed designs. For example, plot scores on a rocket ship to "blast off" toward fluency.

Supporting Diverse Learners

1. **Struggling Readers**
   Celebrate small gains and provide simplified texts to build confidence. Offer one-on-one support during timed readings.
2. **Advanced Readers**
   Encourage advanced students to focus on improving expression, tackling challenging texts, or graphing multiple fluency metrics.
3. **English Language Learners (ELLs)**
   Incorporate bilingual supports, visuals, or culturally relevant texts to make fluency graphing accessible and engaging.

Benefits Beyond Fluency

Fluency graphing reinforces critical skills and encourages habits that extend beyond reading:

- **Self-Reflection:** Students learn to analyze their performance and take ownership of their growth.
- **Perseverance:** Consistent practice develops resilience and fosters a growth mindset.
- **Goal Setting:** Students cultivate the ability to set, pursue, and achieve realistic goals.

Troubleshooting Common Challenges

1. **What if progress is slow?**
   Highlight even small improvements and focus on aspects like accuracy or expression to keep students motivated.
2. **What if students lose interest?**
   Gamify the process by introducing badges, rewards, or themed graphing activities.
3. **What if graphing feels overwhelming?**
   Simplify by pre-labeling graphs or completing the process as a class until students feel comfortable.

Incorporating Fluency Graphing Into Daily Routines

- **Morning Fluency Checks:** Start the day with a quick one-minute timed reading and graph the results.
- **Weekly Progress Monitoring:** Dedicate time each week to fluency graphing as part of literacy instruction.
- **Celebration Days:** Schedule special days to review graphs, reflect on progress, and celebrate achievements.

Lesson Plan 1: Introduction to Fluency Graphing

Grade Level: Appropriate for Grades 3-5

Objective
Students will understand the purpose and benefits of fluency graphing and learn how to conduct a timed reading and graph their Words Per Minute (WPM).

Materials Needed

- Copies of grade-level reading passages
- Stopwatch or timer (one per pair of students)
- Blank fluency graphs with labeled axes (dates on x-axis, WPM on y-axis)
- Pencils and erasers

Time Required
45 minutes

Opening Script
"Today, we're starting an exciting project that will help you see how much your reading improves over time. Have you ever wondered how fast or accurately you read? With fluency graphing, we'll measure how many words you can read correctly in one minute and watch your progress as you practice. This isn't a race—it's about improving little by little and celebrating your hard work!"

Definition of New Concept
Fluency Graphing: A way to track your reading progress by measuring how many words you can read correctly in one minute (WPM) and charting it on a graph to visualize growth.

Activity Directions

1. Pair students and distribute the reading passages, timers, and fluency graphs.
2. *"One of you will read aloud while the other times and counts the number of words read correctly in one minute. Then, you'll switch roles."*
3. Demonstrate how to count WPM and plot the score on the graph. *"For example, if you read 52 words in one minute, you'll find 52 on the graph and plot it under today's date."*
4. Have students conduct their timed readings, record their scores, and plot their first data point on the graph.
5. *"As you practice weekly, you'll see your graph grow, showing how much your reading fluency improves!"*

Assessment
Observe pairs to ensure accurate timing, counting, and graphing. Check completed graphs to verify WPM scores and correct placement of data points.

Intervention
For struggling readers, provide simplified texts and encourage them to focus on accuracy rather than speed. Celebrate small achievements to build confidence.

Enrichment Extension Activity
Advanced readers can create dual graphs, one tracking WPM and the other tracking accuracy scores (e.g., the number of words read correctly divided by total words attempted).

Lesson Plan 2: Setting Goals and Analyzing Progress

Grade Level: Appropriate for Grades 3-5

Objective
Students will set realistic fluency goals, analyze their progress, and reflect on strategies for improvement.

Materials Needed

- Completed fluency graphs (from Lesson 1)
- Sticky notes
- Goal-setting worksheet (with prompts for setting WPM and fluency-related goals)
- Markers or crayons

Time Required
40 minutes

Opening Script
"Now that we've started charting your fluency, it's time to think about where we're headed! Today, we'll set goals for how you'd like to improve your reading and explore ways to make those goals happen. Remember, progress isn't always fast, but every small step counts!"

Definition of New Concept
Goal Setting: The process of deciding on something you want to achieve and planning how to make it happen.

Activity Directions

1. Hand out fluency graphs and encourage students to look at their current scores.
2. *"Take a moment to think about how much you'd like to improve over the next two weeks. What's a number that feels realistic but challenging for you?"*
3. Ask students to brainstorm one realistic WPM goal for the next two weeks and write it on a sticky note to place on their graph.
4. Guide students to complete a goal-setting worksheet, including:
    - *"My current WPM score is ___."*
    - *"My goal for two weeks is ___."*
    - *"To improve, I will: (e.g., practice reading at home, focus on accuracy, use expression)."*
5. Pair students to share their goals and brainstorm additional strategies.
6. End with a class discussion about the importance of persistence and celebrating progress. *"Why do you think it's important to set goals, even if the progress feels small?"*

Assessment
Collect and review goal-setting worksheets to ensure students set achievable and meaningful goals. Observe peer discussions for engagement.

Intervention
Work one-on-one with students struggling to set goals, helping them focus on small, attainable improvements.

Enrichment Extension Activity
Challenge advanced readers to analyze trends in their fluency graphs (e.g., *"What patterns do you notice? How can you maintain or accelerate your progress?"*).

Lesson Plan 3: Celebrating Growth with a Fluency Showcase

Grade Level: Appropriate for Grades 3-5

Objective
Students will reflect on their fluency progress and celebrate their achievements by sharing their graphs and reading aloud to demonstrate growth.

Materials Needed

- Completed fluency graphs
- Certificates of achievement
- A timer for optional one-minute readings during the showcase
- Simple props (e.g., a "podium" for presentations)

Time Required
50 minutes

Opening Script
"Today is all about celebrating YOU and the progress you've made in your reading fluency! You've worked hard, practiced regularly, and tracked your growth. Let's take some time to share our achievements and cheer each other on."

Activity Directions

1. Begin by asking students to look at their graphs and reflect on how their scores have changed. *"What do you notice about your progress? How have you improved?"*
2. Invite each student to share their graph with the class, explaining one challenge they overcame and one thing they're proud of.
3. Optionally, allow students to perform a one-minute timed reading of a passage to showcase their fluency skills. *"This is your chance to show off how far you've come!"*
4. Present certificates of achievement to each student, highlighting their unique progress. *"Congratulations on your hard work and dedication. You should be proud of what you've achieved!"*
5. Conclude with a group reflection on how graphing and goal-setting helped them grow as readers. *"How did graphing your progress make you feel? What would you tell someone just starting their fluency graphing journey?"*

Assessment
Assess participation during the showcase and reflections shared by students about their progress and challenges.

Intervention
Provide a script or prompts for students who feel nervous about presenting their graphs. Pair struggling readers with a supportive peer to share their progress together.

Enrichment Extension Activity
Encourage advanced readers to create a presentation analyzing their progress, including factors that contributed to their growth (e.g., daily practice, challenging texts).

Conclusion

Fluency graphing is a simple yet transformative tool for motivating students and tracking their growth as readers. By visualizing their progress, students develop confidence, a sense of achievement, and the drive to continue improving.

Whether starting at 30 WPM or working toward 100 WPM, every student can experience success through fluency graphing. Each plotted point represents effort, growth, and a step closer to fluent, confident reading. This strategy empowers students to see their potential and builds a solid foundation for lifelong literacy.

Chapter 20

Consistency is Key: Daily Independent Reading

Daily independent reading is a cornerstone of fluency development, offering students the opportunity to practice reading consistently in a low-pressure, enjoyable way. By allowing students to select books they find interesting, this strategy not only builds fluency but also fosters a lifelong love of reading. With regular, uninterrupted time for independent reading, students develop the habits, confidence, and skills needed to become fluent and expressive readers.

Grounded in the science of reading, daily independent reading emphasizes the importance of consistent practice, motivation, and autonomy in fluency development. This chapter explores how to structure independent reading time, the benefits it offers, and strategies to ensure it supports fluency effectively.

The Science Behind Daily Independent Reading

Fluency requires frequent exposure to text, opportunities for practice, and engagement with a variety of reading materials. According to the science of reading, independent reading supports these elements by:

1. **Encouraging Automaticity**
   Regular practice helps students recognize words more quickly, improving their accuracy and speed.
2. **Fostering Motivation**
   Allowing students to choose their own books increases engagement, making reading a positive and enjoyable experience.
3. **Strengthening Comprehension**
   Independent reading builds vocabulary and background knowledge, which are essential for understanding and interpreting text.
4. **Building Reading Stamina**
   Daily reading time helps students develop the focus and endurance needed for sustained, fluent reading.

Why Use Daily Independent Reading for Fluency?

1. **Reinforces Skills**
   Consistent practice with text allows students to apply phonics, decoding, and fluency skills in context.
2. **Promotes Choice and Autonomy**
   Allowing students to select their own books empowers them and increases their intrinsic motivation to read.
3. **Develops a Reading Habit**
   Daily reading builds the habit of consistent practice, which is essential for long-term fluency development.
4. **Supports All Readers**
   Independent reading time can be tailored to meet the needs of diverse learners, from struggling readers to advanced students.

How to Implement Daily Independent Reading

1. **Create a Classroom Library**
   Stock your library with a variety of high-interest books at different reading levels, including fiction, nonfiction, graphic novels, and poetry.
2. **Set Aside Dedicated Time**
   Schedule at least 15 minutes of uninterrupted reading time each day. Consistency is key to building fluency.
3. **Model Independent Reading**
   During reading time, model good reading habits by reading alongside your students. This shows them that reading is a valued and enjoyable activity.
4. **Provide Guidance on Book Selection**
   Help students choose books that align with their interests and reading levels. Use tools like the "Five-Finger Rule" to ensure the book is neither too easy nor too challenging.
5. **Encourage Accountability**
   Use reading logs, journals, or quick reflections to encourage students to track their progress and share their thoughts about what they're reading.

Example Activity: Daily Independent Reading Routine

Step 1: Set up a classroom library with a range of books, such as:

- Fiction: *Diary of a Wimpy Kid, Charlotte's Web*
- Nonfiction: *National Geographic Kids*

- Graphic Novels: *Dog Man, Amulet*

Step 2: Allow students to select a book and find a comfortable reading spot.

Step 3: Set a timer for 15 minutes of uninterrupted silent reading. During this time, read alongside your students to model good habits.

Step 4: After reading, have students complete a quick activity, such as writing a sentence about their favorite part or sharing a prediction about what will happen next.

Variations of Daily Independent Reading

1. **Book Talks**
   Allow students to give brief presentations about their favorite books, encouraging peer recommendations and fostering a sense of community.
2. **Partner Reading**
   Occasionally pair students to read together, alternating pages or discussing the book as they go.
3. **Reading Challenges**
   Set class-wide or individual reading goals, such as completing a certain number of books or pages each month.
4. **Themed Reading Days**
   Create themed days where students choose books related to a specific topic, such as animals, space, or historical events.

Supporting Diverse Learners

1. **Struggling Readers**
   Provide access to high-interest, low-level books and support them in choosing manageable texts. Offer audiobooks to build fluency through listening.
2. **Advanced Readers**
   Challenge advanced students with longer or more complex books and encourage them to explore diverse genres.
3. **English Language Learners (ELLs)**
   Include bilingual books and texts with visual supports to aid comprehension.

Monitoring Progress During Independent Reading

1. **Reading Conferences**
   Hold one-on-one or small-group conferences to discuss students' books, fluency, and overall reading progress.
2. **Fluency Check-ins**
   Periodically have students read a short passage aloud to monitor their pace, accuracy, and expression.
3. **Reading Logs and Journals**
   Encourage students to track the books they've read and reflect on their favorite parts, characters, or themes.

Benefits Beyond Fluency

Daily independent reading develops fluency while also fostering:

- **Comprehension:** Students build vocabulary and knowledge by engaging with diverse texts.
- **Confidence:** Regular practice builds students' self-assurance in their reading abilities.
- **Lifelong Habits:** Students develop a love of reading that extends beyond the classroom.

Troubleshooting Common Challenges

1. **What if students struggle to stay focused?**
   - Start with shorter reading sessions and gradually increase the time. Provide a quiet, comfortable space free from distractions.
2. **What if students don't know what to read?**
   - Offer book recommendations, display "featured books" in the classroom, and use peer suggestions to guide selections.
3. **What if students choose books that are too difficult?**
   - Guide them toward appropriate texts and encourage a mix of easy and challenging books to build confidence and skills.

Incorporating Independent Reading Into Daily Routines

- **Morning Warm-Up:** Begin the day with 10–15 minutes of silent reading.
- **Literacy Block:** Include independent reading as a core part of your daily literacy instruction.
- **End-of-Day Wind-Down:** Use reading time as a calming transition before dismissal.

Lesson Plan 1: Setting Up Independent Reading Routines

Grade Level: 2nd-5th Grade
Objective: Students will understand the purpose and expectations of daily independent reading and select books aligned with their interests and reading levels.

Materials Needed:

- Classroom library with a variety of books (fiction, nonfiction, graphic novels, poetry)
- Reading logs
- "Five-Finger Rule" bookmarks or posters

Time Required: 30 minutes

Opening Script:
"Did you know that reading every day is one of the best ways to become a great reader? Today, we're starting something exciting—our daily independent reading time! This is your chance to explore new worlds, learn amazing things, and practice your reading skills at your own pace."

Define New Concepts (Script):

- **Independent Reading:** *"This is a quiet time when everyone reads their own book. You choose something you love, find a cozy spot, and enjoy reading!"*
- **Five-Finger Rule:** *"When you're picking a book, open to a page and read it. If you find five words that are too hard, the book might be too tricky for now. Try another book."*

Activity Directions:

1. **Introduction to the Classroom Library:**
   - Show students the different sections of the library (fiction, nonfiction, poetry, etc.).
   - Highlight a few "featured books" to generate excitement.
2. **Guided Book Selection:**
   - Teach students the Five-Finger Rule and help them choose books aligned with their interests and reading levels.
3. **Establish Reading Expectations:**

   - Discuss the rules for independent reading time (e.g., read silently, stay focused, take care of books).
4. **Practice Independent Reading:**
   - Allow students to read their chosen book for 10 minutes.
5. **Reflect and Log:**
   - Have students write the title of their book in their reading log and jot down one thing they liked about it.

Assessment:

- Observe students' engagement during reading and ensure they can explain why they chose their book.
- Review reading logs for completeness.

Intervention:

- Help struggling readers find high-interest, low-level books and provide one-on-one support during book selection.

Enrichment/Extension:

- Encourage advanced readers to set goals for completing a certain number of books or exploring new genres.

Lesson Plan 2: Building Reading Stamina

Grade Level: 3rd-5th Grade
Objective: Students will practice sustaining focus during independent reading and reflect on their progress.

Materials Needed:

- Students' chosen books
- Stopwatch or timer
- Reflection journals

Time Required: 35 minutes

Opening Script:
"Last time, we started our independent reading routine. Today, we're going to work on something really important—reading stamina! This means being able to read for longer periods without losing focus. Let's see how long we can read today!"

Define New Concepts (Script):

- **Reading Stamina:** *"This is the ability to keep reading for a longer time without getting distracted. The more you practice, the stronger your stamina becomes—just like a muscle!"*

Activity Directions:

1. **Warm-Up:**
   - Begin with a group discussion: *"What makes it hard to stay focused while reading? How can we avoid distractions?"*
2. **Timed Independent Reading:**
   - Set a timer for 15 minutes. Encourage students to stay focused and enjoy their book.
   - Gradually increase the time each week as stamina improves.
3. **Reflection:**
   - After reading, ask: *"How did it feel to read for 15 minutes? Did you stay focused? What helped you?"*

   - Have students write about their experience in a reflection journal.
4. **Goal Setting:**
   - Encourage students to set a personal goal for improving their stamina (e.g., "Next time, I'll read for 20 minutes without distractions").

Assessment:

- Monitor students' focus during reading time.
- Review reflection journals to assess students' self-awareness and goal-setting.

Intervention:

- Provide struggling readers with shorter reading intervals and gradually increase their time. Offer praise for small improvements.

Enrichment/Extension:

- Advanced readers can challenge themselves with longer books or set a goal to complete a certain number of pages.

Lesson Plan 3: Celebrating Reading Progress

Grade Level: 2nd-5th Grade
Objective: Students will reflect on their independent reading progress and celebrate their achievements.

Materials Needed:

- Students' reading logs
- Certificates or bookmarks for recognition
- Chart paper or digital tools for class-wide book totals

Time Required: 40 minutes

Opening Script:
"You've all been working hard during our independent reading time, and it's time to celebrate! Today, we'll look back at what we've accomplished, share our favorite books, and set new goals for the next month."

Define New Concepts (Script):

- **Reflection:** *"This means looking back at what you've done and thinking about what you've learned or enjoyed."*
- **Celebration:** *"It's important to celebrate our hard work and feel proud of what we've achieved!"*

Activity Directions:

1. **Review Reading Logs:**
    - Have students count the number of books or pages they've read so far.
    - Ask: *"What was your favorite book or part of your reading journey?"*
2. **Share and Celebrate:**
    - Allow students to share their favorite book or reading moment with the class.
    - Recognize achievements with certificates or bookmarks (e.g., "Most Pages Read" or "Best Genre Explorer").
3. **Set New Goals:**

- Discuss as a class: *"What do we want to accomplish next? How can we make our reading time even better?"*
- Have students write a goal in their reading log (e.g., "I want to read three books next month").

Assessment:

- Review students' reading logs to track progress.
- Listen to class discussions for insights into their engagement and growth.

Intervention:

- For students with less progress, provide encouragement and suggest specific books or strategies to reignite their interest.

Enrichment/Extension:

- Challenge advanced readers to write a short review or recommendation for their favorite book to share with peers.

These plans ensure daily independent reading is structured, meaningful, and motivating, fostering fluency development and a love for reading.

Conclusion

Daily independent reading is an essential component of fluency instruction, providing students with consistent opportunities to practice reading in a meaningful and enjoyable way. By allowing students to choose books that interest them, this strategy fosters a love of reading while building the skills needed for fluent, confident, and lifelong literacy.

Whether students are diving into the humorous world of *Diary of a Wimpy Kid* or exploring the adventures of *Dog Man*, independent reading helps fluency flow naturally. With every page turned, students grow as readers, thinkers, and learners, one book at a time.

Chapter 21

Dramas and Fluency: Bringing Reading to Life

Drama is a powerful tool for developing reading fluency, offering students the opportunity to practice expressive, purposeful reading while engaging deeply with text. Scripts provide a unique format that encourages natural pacing, accurate intonation, and clear expression—all essential components of fluency. Unlike standard prose, scripts include dialogue, stage directions, and background information, requiring students to think critically about how tone, mood, and context influence their delivery.

Through drama, students not only build fluency but also gain confidence in reading aloud and interpreting text. Starting with simple scripts in elementary school and progressing to more complex plays in high school, drama integrates seamlessly into fluency instruction, helping students develop skills that extend beyond the classroom.

The Role of Stage Directions in Fluency

In dramas, stage directions—often written in brackets or italics—offer essential guidance for understanding a character's actions, tone, and motivations. These instructions provide critical context that shapes how dialogue is delivered and how the story unfolds.

For example:

- *[Angrily, slamming the door]*
- *[Whispering nervously]*
- *[The lights dim as the storm begins outside]*

Stage directions influence:

1. **Mood and Tone:** A line spoken *angrily* differs significantly from one spoken *nervously.* Recognizing these cues helps students read with appropriate emotion and expression.
2. **Characterization:** Directions provide insights into a character's feelings, relationships, and personality, enabling students to deliver dialogue authentically.

3. **Setting and Reactions:** Details about the environment or other characters' responses help students visualize the scene, affecting how they interpret and perform their lines.
4. **Plot Development:** Stage directions guide how the story progresses, helping students understand how their delivery contributes to the overall narrative.

By paying close attention to what is within brackets, students learn to read beyond the words, engaging with text on a deeper level and making their fluency more natural and purposeful.

Why Dramas Improve Fluency

1. **Encourages Expression:** Dramas require students to vary their tone, pitch, and pacing to reflect the emotions and intentions of the characters.
2. **Fosters Engagement:** Performing scripts makes reading interactive and enjoyable, motivating students to practice fluency.
3. **Supports Comprehension:** Interpreting stage directions and dialogue helps students understand how tone and context contribute to meaning.
4. **Builds Confidence:** Acting out scenes in a safe, supportive environment allows students to take risks and grow as readers.

How to Incorporate Drama into Fluency Instruction

1. **Choose Appropriate Scripts**
   Select scripts or scenes that match students' reading levels and interests. Start with short, simple dialogues and gradually progress to longer, more complex pieces.
   Examples:
   - Elementary: *The Three Little Pigs*
   - Middle School: *A Christmas Carol*
   - High School: *Romeo and Juliet*
2. **Model Fluency**
   Read a section of the script aloud, demonstrating how to interpret stage directions and deliver lines with proper pacing, emotion, and emphasis.
3. **Practice in Small Groups**
   Divide students into groups to rehearse scenes. Encourage them to focus on how stage directions affect their delivery and how characters interact.
4. **Perform for an Audience**
   Allow students to perform their scenes for classmates or even parents, emphasizing expression and clarity.
5. **Reflect and Provide Feedback**
   After performances, discuss what worked well and what could be improved. Highlight how attention to stage directions enhanced the delivery.

Example Activity: Script Practice

Step 1: Provide a short script, such as a scene from *The Three Little Pigs.*

- *Wolf: [Growling loudly] Little pig, little pig, let me in!*
- *Pig: [Shaking] Not by the hair on my chinny chin chin!*

Step 2: Model how to read the lines, emphasizing the tone suggested by the stage directions.

Step 3: Have students rehearse in pairs or groups, focusing on how their delivery reflects the stage directions.

Step 4: Perform the scene for the class and discuss how the stage directions influenced the mood and tone.

Variations of Drama Activities

1. **Reader's Theater**
   Students read scripts aloud without memorizing lines, focusing entirely on fluency and expression.
2. **Improvised Stage Directions**
   Challenge students to add their own stage directions to a script, encouraging creativity and deeper comprehension.
3. **Script Writing**
   Have students write short scripts, including detailed stage directions, to perform with their peers.
4. **Thematic Plays**
   Use plays that align with curriculum topics, such as historical events or literature themes, to enhance cross-curricular learning.

Supporting Diverse Learners

1. **Struggling Readers**
   Provide scripts with fewer lines or simpler language. Pair them with stronger readers for support.
2. **Advanced Readers**
   Challenge advanced students with complex characters or roles requiring nuanced interpretation.

3. **English Language Learners (ELLs)**
   Use scripts with visuals or simplified stage directions to support comprehension and fluency.

Benefits Beyond Fluency

Dramas not only improve fluency but also:

- **Enhance Comprehension:** Students gain a deeper understanding of text by analyzing tone, mood, and characterization.
- **Build Collaboration:** Performing scenes fosters teamwork and communication.
- **Encourage Creativity:** Students explore their imaginative side through acting and interpretation.

Troubleshooting Common Challenges

1. **What if students feel shy or embarrassed?**
   - Start with smaller groups or use reader's theater to build confidence.
2. **What if students struggle with stage directions?**
   - Spend time discussing the meaning of specific instructions and modeling how to incorporate them into reading.
3. **What if performances lack expression?**
   - Practice lines repeatedly, focusing on how tone and pacing affect meaning.

Incorporating Drama into Daily Routines

- **Morning Fluency Warm-Up:** Begin the day with a short scene or dialogue.
- **Literacy Centers:** Include drama scripts as part of your fluency stations.
- **Weekly Performances:** Dedicate time each week for students to rehearse and perform a scene.

Lesson Plan 1: Introducing Stage Directions in Drama

Grade Level: 3rd–5th Grade
Objective: Students will understand the role of stage directions in scripts and practice using them to guide their reading fluency.

Materials Needed:

- Script excerpts from *The Three Little Pigs* or a similar simple play
- Chart paper or whiteboard to define terms
- Highlighters or colored pencils

Time Required: 30 minutes

Opening Script:
"Have you ever noticed how actors in movies or plays seem to know exactly how to show what their characters are feeling? That's because they follow something called stage directions! Today, we'll learn how these directions help us read and perform with expression."

Define New Concepts (Script):

- **Stage Directions:** *"These are instructions in a script that tell actors how to move, speak, or act. They're usually in brackets or italics. For example, if it says [angrily], the character is supposed to sound upset."*
- **Fluency and Expression:** *"When we read aloud, we use our voices to show the emotions and actions in the story. Stage directions are like clues that help us do this."*

Activity Directions:

1. **Introduction to Stage Directions:**
    - Show an example: *Wolf: [Growling loudly] Little pig, little pig, let me in!*
    - Highlight the bracketed words and discuss what they mean.
2. **Guided Practice:**
    - Pass out script excerpts.
    - As a class, highlight stage directions and discuss how they should affect the delivery of the lines.
3. **Small Group Practice:**

   - In groups of three or four, students take turns reading lines aloud, incorporating stage directions for expression.
4. **Reflection:**
   - Ask: *"How did the stage directions change the way you read? Did it feel different from regular reading?"*

Assessment:

- Observe students' ability to follow stage directions during group practice.

Intervention:

- Provide struggling readers with simpler scripts or pair them with a confident peer for support.

Enrichment/Extension:

- Have advanced students rewrite stage directions for the same scene, experimenting with different emotions.

Lesson Plan 2: Reader's Theater with Expression

Grade Level: 4th–6th Grade
Objective: Students will practice fluency and expression through a Reader's Theater performance.

Materials Needed:

- Scripts for *The Three Little Pigs* or a similar short play
- Props (optional, such as a small door cutout or paper hats for pigs and wolf)
- Fluency checklist (for feedback on tone, pacing, and expression)

Time Required: 40 minutes

Opening Script:
"Today, we're going to become actors in a Reader's Theater! You'll practice reading a script with expression and then perform for the class. Remember, you don't have to memorize anything—just focus on reading fluently and bringing the characters to life."

Define New Concepts (Script):

- **Reader's Theater:** *"This is a type of drama where you read from a script, focusing on your voice and expression instead of memorizing lines or acting out every movement."*
- **Expression in Fluency:** *"Expression means using your voice to show how your character feels. Are they happy, sad, angry, or scared?"*

Activity Directions:

1. **Divide Into Groups:**
   - Assign roles to each student (e.g., narrator, Pig 1, Pig 2, Wolf).
2. **Practice Reading:**
   - Groups read through their scripts multiple times, focusing on fluency and expression.
3. **Performance:**
   - Each group performs their scene for the class. Encourage them to use their voices and gestures to bring the story to life.
4. **Feedback:**

    - After each performance, discuss what worked well and what could improve (e.g., *"I loved how the wolf sounded scary!"*).

Assessment:

- Use a fluency checklist to evaluate students on pacing, tone, and expression during the performance.

Intervention:

- Provide one-on-one practice time for students struggling with expression or pacing.

Enrichment/Extension:

- Have students create a new scene or add dialogue to the existing script.

Lesson Plan 3: Creating and Performing Original Scripts

Grade Level: 5th–8th Grade
Objective: Students will write and perform their own short scripts, incorporating stage directions and expressive dialogue.

Materials Needed:

- Blank script templates
- Markers or colored pencils for illustrating scenes
- Example script with clear stage directions

Time Required: 45 minutes

Opening Script:
"Imagine you could write your own play! What would the characters say? How would they act? Today, you'll become scriptwriters and performers, creating a short scene that includes dialogue and stage directions."

Define New Concepts (Script):

- **Scriptwriting:** *"A script tells a story through dialogue and stage directions. It's like a playbook for actors!"*
- **Collaboration in Drama:** *"When we work together on a play, we share ideas and listen to each other. This makes our scenes even better!"*

Activity Directions:

1. **Brainstorm Ideas:**
    - In small groups, students brainstorm a setting, characters, and a simple conflict for their script (e.g., a lost treasure, a school adventure).
2. **Write the Script:**
    - Groups write 4–6 lines of dialogue, including at least two stage directions (e.g., *[laughing nervously]* or *[pointing to the treasure chest]*).
3. **Rehearse:**
    - Groups practice reading their scripts aloud, focusing on fluency and expression.
4. **Perform:**

   - Each group performs their scene for the class.
5. **Feedback:**
   - Classmates provide positive feedback on creativity and expression.

Assessment:

- Evaluate scripts for inclusion of stage directions and fluency during performances.

Intervention:

- Provide sentence starters or prompts for groups struggling to write dialogue.

Enrichment/Extension:

- Advanced groups can add a second scene or write an alternate ending.

These drama-based lessons encourage fluency, creativity, and collaboration while making reading a dynamic, interactive experience.

Conclusion

Dramas bring text to life, turning reading into an interactive and expressive experience. By teaching students to interpret and deliver dialogue with attention to stage directions, you help them develop fluency that feels natural, purposeful, and engaging.

From simple scenes to full-scale productions, incorporating drama into your classroom fosters confidence, creativity, and a love for reading. When students perform, fluency flows—and with it comes a deeper connection to the stories they read and share.

Chapter 22

Memorization: The Missing Link to Fluency Today

Memorization, once a cornerstone of education, has become an overlooked but invaluable tool in building reading fluency. A generation ago, students routinely memorized meaningful texts—such as the Preamble to the Constitution, famous speeches, or classic poems—and recited them in public. This practice didn't just ensure short-term recall; it cultivated fluency, confidence, and an appreciation for the rhythm and expression of language. Through repeated practice and public recitation, students became adept at understanding and delivering text with natural pacing, proper inflection, and meaningful tone.

Memorization's influence extends beyond recitation. The journey of internalizing and performing a text requires students to deeply engage with its meaning, phrasing, and emotional cues. These skills transfer directly to both silent and oral reading, improving comprehension, self-expression, and confidence. By reintroducing memorization as a fluency-building strategy, educators can help students master not only the text but also the lifelong skills of clear, confident communication.

The Role of Memorization in Fluency

1. **Fosters Expressive Delivery**
   Memorizing and reciting text repeatedly encourages students to consider tone, pacing, and volume to convey meaning.
2. **Builds Reading Stamina and Confidence**
   The act of performing memorized text in front of peers strengthens both fluency and self-assurance, helping students become more comfortable with reading aloud.
3. **Reinforces Long-Term Retention**
   Memorization ensures that important language patterns, vocabulary, and phrasing are deeply embedded in students' minds, supporting comprehension and fluency over time.
4. **Improves Silent Reading Skills**
   When students internalize text through memorization, they naturally apply inflection and expression to their silent reading, enriching their understanding of tone and mood.

How Memorization Enhances Fluency

The process of memorization requires students to break text into meaningful chunks, focus on phrasing, and practice delivery with expression. Each of these steps directly supports fluency by:

- **Improving Pacing:** Students learn to slow down or speed up depending on the emotional weight or urgency of the text.
- **Enhancing Intonation:** Memorizing and performing texts teaches students to adjust their tone to reflect a character's mood or the message of the piece.
- **Strengthening Rhythm:** Repeated practice helps students develop a natural flow in their reading.

Example:
Consider the line from Dr. Martin Luther King Jr.'s "I Have a Dream" speech:

- *"I have a dream that one day every valley shall be exalted, every hill and mountain shall be made low."*
    - The phrase "I have a dream" is best delivered with deliberate pacing and rising intonation, emphasizing its hopeful tone.
    - The repetition of "every" calls for a steady rhythm, building momentum toward the powerful conclusion.

Practical Applications of Memorization in the Classroom

1. **Start with Short Texts**
   Begin with manageable pieces such as poems, famous quotes, or short passages from speeches.
   Examples:
    - *"Four score and seven years ago..."* (Abraham Lincoln)
    - *"The woods are lovely, dark, and deep..."* (Robert Frost)
2. **Guide Students Through Analysis**
   Before memorizing, help students break down the text to understand its meaning, tone, and phrasing.
3. **Model Proper Delivery**
   Demonstrate how to vary pacing, tone, and volume to convey the message effectively. For example:
    - A question might end with rising intonation (*"Shall I compare thee to a summer's day?"*).
    - A serious statement might call for slower pacing and a firm tone (*"We hold these truths to be self-evident..."*).

4. **Encourage Repetition**
   Allow students to practice repeatedly, focusing first on accuracy, then on expression and fluency.
5. **Provide Opportunities for Performance**
   Have students recite their memorized text in small groups or in front of the class. Celebrate their efforts to build confidence.

Benefits of Memorization Beyond Fluency

Memorization offers far-reaching benefits that extend into other areas of academic and personal growth:

- **Improved Comprehension:** Analyzing the text for meaning during memorization strengthens understanding.
- **Public Speaking Skills:** Reciting text aloud builds confidence in speaking clearly and expressively.
- **Lifelong Retention:** Students internalize meaningful language and ideas that stay with them into adulthood.
- **Cultural Literacy:** Memorizing foundational texts exposes students to important historical and literary works.

Supporting Diverse Learners

1. **Struggling Readers:** Start with shorter, simpler texts and provide additional modeling and guidance. Celebrate small successes.
2. **Advanced Readers:** Challenge them with longer passages or more complex texts, encouraging nuanced delivery.
3. **English Language Learners (ELLs):** Choose texts with clear, repetitive language and provide visuals to aid comprehension.

Example Activity: Memorization for Fluency

Step 1: Select a short poem, such as Robert Frost's *Stopping by Woods on a Snowy Evening.*

Step 2: Read the poem aloud, modeling fluency and expression. Discuss the mood and tone of each stanza.

Step 3: Break the poem into chunks and have students practice one section at a time, focusing on pacing and intonation.

Step 4: Over the course of a week, students memorize the poem, practicing with peers or in small groups.

Step 5: Host a poetry recitation day, allowing students to perform their memorized pieces for the class.

Lesson Plan 1: Introduction to Memorization for Fluency

Grade Level: 4th–6th Grade
Objective: Students will understand how memorization supports fluency and begin memorizing a short, meaningful text.

Materials Needed:

- Copies of a short poem or speech excerpt (e.g., "Four score and seven years ago…" or Robert Frost's *Stopping by Woods on a Snowy Evening*)
- Chart paper for breaking text into sections
- Highlighters or colored pencils

Time Required: 30 minutes

Opening Script:
"Have you ever learned a song by heart? When we memorize something, like a favorite tune or poem, we understand it deeply and can perform it with confidence. Today, we'll explore how memorizing text can make us better, more expressive readers."

Define New Concepts (Script):

- **Memorization:** *"This is when we learn something so well that we can say it without looking. It helps us focus on tone, rhythm, and expression because we don't need to worry about decoding the words."*
- **Fluency:** *"Fluency is how smoothly and expressively we read. Memorizing text helps us practice reading with confidence and clarity."*

Activity Directions:

1. **Model the Process:**
   - Read the selected text aloud, demonstrating proper pacing, tone, and expression.
   - Discuss how the tone changes throughout the piece.
2. **Break It Down:**
   - Divide the text into manageable chunks (e.g., lines or sentences).
   - Highlight key phrases or words that should be emphasized.
3. **Practice Repetition:**

   - Have students read the first chunk aloud as a group, mimicking your expression.
   - Repeat the chunk until they can read it fluently.
4. **Independent Practice:**
   - Allow students to practice the chunk quietly or with a partner.
5. **Reflection:**
   - Ask: *"How does focusing on tone and rhythm change the way you understand this text?"*

Assessment:

- Observe students during group and partner practice to evaluate their pacing, expression, and confidence.

Intervention:

- Provide additional modeling and one-on-one practice for students struggling with expression or accuracy.

Enrichment/Extension:

- Challenge advanced students to memorize an additional stanza or write a brief reflection on how the text's tone influences its meaning.

Lesson Plan 2: Deep Dive into Text Analysis

Grade Level: 5th–8th Grade
Objective: Students will analyze a text for tone, rhythm, and phrasing to aid memorization and fluency.

Materials Needed:

- Excerpts from Martin Luther King Jr.'s "I Have a Dream" or a similar speech
- Vocabulary list with key terms from the text
- Notebooks for annotations

Time Required: 40 minutes

Opening Script:
"When we memorize text, it's not just about repeating words—it's about understanding the meaning behind them. Today, we'll analyze how tone and rhythm bring a text to life, helping us prepare to memorize and perform it fluently."

Define New Concepts (Script):

- **Tone:** *"Tone is how the speaker feels about the topic. For example, in Dr. King's speech, his tone is hopeful and determined."*
- **Rhythm:** *"Rhythm is the flow of the words. Some phrases are slow and deliberate, while others are quick and energetic."*

Activity Directions:

1. **Text Annotation:**
    - Distribute copies of the excerpt.
    - Guide students in identifying key phrases and annotating the text for tone and rhythm. Example:
        - *"I have a dream..." (Hopeful, deliberate)*
        - *"Let freedom ring..." (Excited, rhythmic)*
2. **Model and Practice:**
    - Model reading a line with the identified tone and rhythm.
    - Have students echo your reading.

3. **Partner Practice:**
    - In pairs, students take turns reading the excerpt aloud, focusing on their annotated tone and rhythm.
4. **Reflection:**
    - Discuss: *"How does understanding the tone change the way you read this text?"*

Assessment:

- Evaluate students' ability to identify tone and apply it during partner reading.

Intervention:

- Provide sentence frames or examples for students struggling to analyze tone.

Enrichment/Extension:

- Have advanced students write a short paragraph about how rhythm and tone contribute to the overall message of the text.

Lesson Plan 3: Performance and Recitation

Grade Level: 6th–8th Grade
Objective: Students will confidently recite memorized text with accurate pacing, tone, and expression.

Materials Needed:

- Memorized text (e.g., a stanza of "I Have a Dream" or *Stopping by Woods on a Snowy Evening*)
- Feedback rubrics for peers and teachers
- Small props for added engagement (optional)

Time Required: 45 minutes

Opening Script:
"Today is performance day! You've practiced and memorized your text, and now it's time to share it. Remember, your goal is to use your voice to bring the words to life and connect with your audience."

Define New Concepts (Script):

- **Public Speaking Skills:** *"When reciting text, speak clearly, make eye contact, and use your tone to show meaning."*
- **Constructive Feedback:** *"We'll listen to each other's performances and give positive, helpful feedback to improve our skills."*

Activity Directions:

1. **Rehearsal:**
   - Students rehearse their recitations in pairs or small groups, providing feedback to one another.
2. **Performance:**
   - Each student performs their memorized text for the class.
   - Use a rubric to evaluate pacing, tone, and expression.
3. **Feedback Session:**

   - After each performance, peers share one strength and one suggestion for improvement.
4. **Celebrate Achievements:**
   - End the session with applause and recognition for all participants.

Assessment:

- Use the rubric to assess students' fluency, tone, and expression during their recitations.

Intervention:

- Allow students who are nervous about public speaking to recite their text for the teacher or a small group.

Enrichment/Extension:

- Challenge advanced students to recite additional stanzas or perform their text for a different audience, such as another class.

These lessons encourage fluency development while building confidence, comprehension, and appreciation for the power of language.

Conclusion

Memorization is more than an academic exercise—it's a gateway to fluent, expressive reading and confident communication. As students memorize and recite meaningful texts, they internalize the rhythm, tone, and pacing of language, improving both their oral and silent reading fluency.

By reintroducing memorization into today's classrooms, teachers can help students not only master important texts but also develop the skills and self-assurance to read and speak with fluency, expression, and purpose. Through the power of memorization, fluency flows naturally, shaping readers who are prepared to engage with language and ideas for a lifetime.

Chapter 23

What Exactly Did You Say?

Reading fluency goes beyond pacing and accuracy—it includes understanding how vocal stress impacts meaning. The way a reader emphasizes certain words in a sentence can completely change its interpretation. This concept is vital for fluency, as it helps students move beyond mere word recognition to truly expressing and understanding the text.

In this chapter, we'll explore how placing stress on different words within the same sentence alters its meaning. We'll break down examples across various parts of speech, showing how emphasis affects interpretation. By teaching students to recognize and apply stress effectively, you can enhance their reading fluency, comprehension, and ability to convey meaning with precision.

From emphasizing a single word to shifting tone across an entire sentence, stress gives text depth and dimension. With practice, students will not only improve their fluency but also develop a richer understanding of language's power to convey meaning. And as they master the art of stress, their fluency will flow naturally, making their reading—and speaking—clearer and more engaging.

The Power of Stress in a Sentence

Consider the sentence:
"I didn't say she stole my pencil."

By stressing different words, the meaning shifts dramatically:

1. **I** didn't say she stole my pencil.
   - Meaning: Someone else said it, not you.
2. I **didn't** say she stole my pencil.
   - Meaning: You're denying having said it.
3. I didn't **say** she stole my pencil.
   - Meaning: You implied or suggested it but didn't say it outright.
4. I didn't say **she** stole my pencil.

  - Meaning: Someone else (not her) stole the pencil.
5. I didn't say she **stole** my pencil.
   - Meaning: She might have borrowed it, but she didn't steal it.
6. I didn't say she stole **my** pencil.
   - Meaning: She stole someone else's pencil, not yours.
7. I didn't say she stole my **pencil.**
   - Meaning: She stole something else, not the pencil.

These shifts in emphasis demonstrate how vocal stress can dramatically alter meaning. Understanding and practicing this skill helps students read with expression, interpret text accurately, and communicate effectively.

Stress and Parts of Speech

Stress placement varies depending on the word being emphasized and its role in the sentence. Below, we examine how stress changes meaning when placed on different parts of speech:

1. **Nouns**
   - Example: *"The boy kicked the ball."*
     - Stress on **boy**: Emphasizes who performed the action (not the girl).
     - Stress on **ball**: Highlights what was kicked (not a rock or a can).
2. **Verbs**
   - Example: *"She danced gracefully."*
     - Stress on **danced**: Highlights the action she performed (not walked or sang).
     - Stress on **gracefully**: Emphasizes how she danced, focusing on the manner.
3. **Adjectives**
   - Example: *"He wore a red shirt."*
     - Stress on **red**: Emphasizes the color of the shirt (not blue or green).
     - Stress on **shirt**: Shifts focus to what was red (not pants or a hat).
4. **Adverbs**
   - Example: *"They spoke softly."*
     - Stress on **softly**: Emphasizes how they spoke (not loudly or harshly).
     - Stress on **spoke**: Highlights the act of speaking (not writing or yelling).
5. **Pronouns**
   - Example: *"She said he did it."*
     - Stress on **she**: Emphasizes who made the statement (not someone else).
     - Stress on **he**: Points to who was accused of doing it (not someone else).

Practicing Stress in the Classroom

1. **Analyze Sentences**
   Provide students with sentences where they practice stressing different words and discussing how the meaning changes.

   Example Sentence:

   - "The dog chased the cat."
     - Stress on **dog**: Focuses on who did the chasing.
     - Stress on **chased**: Highlights the action performed.
     - Stress on **cat**: Clarifies what was being chased.
2. **Role-Playing Dialogue**
   Assign students roles in a scripted dialogue and encourage them to experiment with stress.
   Example:
   - Line: *"I thought you knew about the surprise."*
     - Stress on **I**: Suggests someone else was supposed to tell them.
     - Stress on **thought**: Indicates uncertainty about their knowledge.
     - Stress on **knew**: Implies surprise at their lack of awareness.
3. **Reader's Theater**
   Use scripts with dialogue and stage directions, prompting students to apply stress to convey emotions, tone, and meaning.
4. **Stress Contrast Drills**
   Provide contrasting sentences and have students practice reading them with the appropriate stress.
   Example:
   - *"She didn't **run** to the store."*
   - *"She didn't run to the **store**."*

Benefits of Stress Practice

Teaching students how to apply stress strategically improves fluency by:

- **Enhancing Comprehension**: Students learn to interpret text more accurately by considering tone and context.
- **Improving Expression**: Stress practice helps students read with natural intonation, making their reading more engaging and authentic.
- **Supporting Oral Communication**: Mastering stress aids in public speaking and conversational skills.

Supporting Diverse Learners

1. **Struggling Readers**
   Use short, simple sentences to introduce stress concepts and provide ample modeling.
2. **Advanced Readers**
   Challenge them with complex sentences or texts where stress alters subtle nuances of meaning.
3. **English Language Learners (ELLs)**
   Focus on sentences with clear, repetitive patterns to help them hear and practice stress differences.

Lesson Plan 1: Exploring the Power of Stress in Sentences

Grade Level: 4th-6th Grades

Objective
Students will understand how placing stress on different words within a sentence alters its meaning and apply this concept to their own reading for better fluency and comprehension.

Materials Needed

- Sentence strips with examples of sentences for stress practice (e.g., *"I didn't say she stole my pencil"*)
- Whiteboard and markers
- Highlighters for students
- Handout: "The Power of Stress in Sentences" (sample sentences with space for notes)

Time Required
45 minutes

Opening Script
"Today, we're going to explore how the way we emphasize certain words in a sentence can completely change what it means. Think about how a sentence like, 'I didn't say she stole my pencil,' can mean so many different things just by stressing different words. By learning this skill, you'll improve your reading fluency, comprehension, and expression. Let's dive in!"

Definition of New Concept
Vocal Stress: The emphasis placed on specific words within a sentence to change or clarify its meaning.

Activity Directions

1. Write the sentence *"I didn't say she stole my pencil"* on the board. Read it aloud, stressing a different word each time. After each reading, ask: *"What does the sentence mean now?"*
   - Example: *"I didn't say she stole my pencil."* (Someone else said it.)
   - Example: *"I didn't say she stole my pencil."* (Maybe you implied it but didn't say it directly.)
2. Distribute the "Power of Stress in Sentences" handout. In pairs, students practice reading sentences aloud, emphasizing different words.
3. After practicing, have pairs share one example with the class and explain how the meaning changed.
4. Conclude with a discussion: *"Why is it important to understand how stress works in sentences? How can this help us in reading and speaking?"*

Assessment
Listen to students as they practice ensuring they are correctly emphasizing words and interpreting meaning changes. Use a quick exit slip where students answer: *"How does vocal stress change the meaning of a sentence?"*

Intervention
Provide struggling readers with simpler sentences and model stress placement multiple times before asking them to practice.

Enrichment Extension Activity
Advanced students can create their own sentences and challenge peers to identify how meaning shifts when stress is placed on different words.

Lesson Plan 2: Practicing Stress in Dialogue

Grade Level: 4th-6th Grades

Objective
Students will apply the concept of vocal stress by practicing stress shifts in scripted dialogue to enhance fluency and expression.

Materials Needed

- Scripted dialogue (short scenes or conversations, e.g., *"I thought you knew about the surprise"*)
- Highlighters and pencils
- Optional: Audio recordings of the dialogue read with different stress placements

Time Required
50 minutes

Opening Script
"Have you ever noticed how the way someone says something changes what they really mean? Today, we'll explore this idea by practicing stress in dialogue. When you read with expression and place stress in the right places, you make conversations and stories come to life. Let's learn how to do that together!"

Definition of New Concept
Stress in Dialogue: The intentional emphasis on specific words within dialogue to convey meaning, emotion, or tone.

Activity Directions

1. Hand out short scripted dialogues. Read one example aloud, modeling stress shifts (e.g., *"I thought you knew about the surprise"*). Highlight stressed words.
2. In pairs, students practice reading the dialogue aloud, experimenting with different stress placements and discussing how meaning changes.
3. Have each pair choose one line from the dialogue to perform for the class, explaining the stress choices they made.
4. Discuss: *"How does using stress make dialogue more engaging and easier to understand?"*

Assessment
Observe student pairs as they practice. Evaluate their performances for appropriate stress placement and expression.

Intervention
Provide visual aids for struggling readers, such as bolded or underlined text, to guide stress placement.

Enrichment Extension Activity
Challenge advanced students to rewrite their dialogue to include stage directions, emphasizing where stress should be placed (e.g., *"I thought (pause) YOU knew about the surprise"*).

Lesson Plan 3: Reader's Theater with Stress

Grade Level: 4th-6th Grades

Objective
Students will use vocal stress to enhance expression and comprehension in a Reader's Theater performance.

Materials Needed

- Short Reader's Theater scripts (with a focus on dialogue)
- Highlighters and pencils
- Certificates for participation

Time Required
60 minutes

Opening Script
"Have you ever heard someone read a story that made you feel like you were right there in the moment? That's the power of reading with stress and expression! Today, we'll use what we've learned about stress to bring characters and dialogue to life in a Reader's Theater performance. Let's make these scripts come alive!"

Definition of New Concept
Reader's Theater: A dramatic reading of a script where the focus is on vocal expression rather than memorization or physical movement.

Activity Directions

1. Distribute scripts and assign roles. In small groups, students read through their parts silently, then aloud, highlighting words where stress is needed.
2. Model a dramatic reading of a line, emphasizing how stress changes tone and meaning. Encourage students to mimic this technique in their own parts.
3. Allow groups to practice together, focusing on stress, tone, and expression.
4. Groups perform their scripts for the class. After each performance, discuss: *"How did their use of stress help convey the characters' emotions or intentions?"*
5. End with certificates of participation and a class reflection: *"What did you learn about stress and expression today? How can this help your reading and speaking in the future?"*

Assessment
Evaluate performances for appropriate stress placement, clear expression, and overall engagement with the text.

Intervention
Support struggling readers by assigning simpler roles or allowing them to work with a partner on their lines.

Enrichment Extension Activity
Advanced students can write their own Reader's Theater scripts, incorporating lines where stress shifts are critical to meaning. These scripts can be performed by peers in a future lesson.

Conclusion

The ability to apply stress effectively is a vital component of fluent reading and communication. By teaching students how stress alters meaning in a sentence, you help them become more expressive, thoughtful readers and speakers.

APPENDIX A

Cross-Curricular Resources

Fluency Passages on Science Concepts

Here are five short fluency passages, each focusing on a key science concept. These passages are designed to help students practice reading fluently while learning about important scientific ideas.

---

1. How Machines Work

Machines make our lives easier by helping us do work. A machine is anything that uses energy to perform a task. Simple machines include levers, pulleys, and inclined planes. For example, a seesaw is a lever that helps lift heavy objects. A pulley, like the one used on a flagpole, makes it easier to raise a flag. Machines use force to move objects or change direction. They save us time and effort, making hard tasks manageable. Can you think of a machine you use every day?

---

2. Life Cycle of a Frog

A frog's life begins as a tiny egg floating in water. Soon, the egg hatches into a tadpole. Tadpoles have long tails and no legs. They swim in ponds or streams, breathing with gills. Over time, the tadpole grows legs, and its tail gets shorter. It becomes a froglet, a small frog with a stubby tail. Finally, the tail disappears, and the frog can hop on land. Adult frogs lay eggs, starting the life cycle all over again. What part of the frog's life cycle do you find the most amazing?

---

3. The Invention of Penicillin

Penicillin was discovered by accident in 1928 by Alexander Fleming. He noticed mold growing on a petri dish in his lab. The mold was killing harmful bacteria! Fleming realized the mold, called Penicillium, could be used to fight infections. Penicillin became the first antibiotic and has saved millions of lives since its discovery. It is used to treat illnesses like pneumonia and strep throat. Imagine how important this discovery was for modern medicine! How might life be different without antibiotics?

---

4. The Scientific Method

The scientific method is a process that helps scientists solve problems. It starts with a question, like, "Why do plants grow faster in sunlight?" Next, scientists make a hypothesis, or an educated guess. Then, they test their hypothesis by doing experiments and collecting data. After analyzing the results, they decide if their hypothesis was correct. If it wasn't, they try again! The scientific method helps us understand the world and make new discoveries. Can you think of a question you'd like to explore using the scientific method?

---

5. Ways to Be Safe in a Science Lab

Safety is the most important rule in a science lab. Always wear safety goggles to protect your eyes. If you handle chemicals, wear gloves to protect your skin. Never taste or touch anything unless your teacher says it's safe. Follow instructions carefully, and don't mix unknown substances. Clean up your workspace when you're done to avoid accidents. By following these safety rules, you can enjoy experiments and learn without getting hurt. What is the most important lab safety rule to remember?

Fluency Passages on Social Studies Concepts

Here are five updated passages designed to help students practice reading fluency while learning about important social studies topics.

---

1. The Invention of the Steam Engine

The invention of the steam engine in the late 1600s and early 1700s revolutionized transportation and industry. Early versions, like Thomas Newcomen's engine, were used to pump water out of mines. Later, James Watt improved the design, making it more efficient and useful for powering machines in factories. The steam engine also played a key role in the development of railroads and steamships, which transformed transportation. Goods could now travel faster and farther, boosting economies and connecting people across great distances. The steam engine was a driving force of the Industrial Revolution.

---

2. The Industrial Revolution

The Industrial Revolution began in the late 1700s and changed how goods were made and how people lived. Before this time, most items were created by hand in homes or small workshops. During the revolution, factories powered by machines like steam engines took over production. These factories made goods faster and cheaper, leading to the growth of cities as people moved to work in urban areas. Transportation also advanced with inventions like railroads and steamships. The Industrial Revolution marked the beginning of modern industry and transformed economies worldwide.

---

3. The Texas Revolution

The Texas Revolution was a fight for independence from Mexico in 1835–1836. Settlers in Texas clashed with the Mexican government over issues like land ownership and government control. One of the most famous events of the revolution was the Battle of the Alamo, where a small group of Texans fought bravely but ultimately lost. Despite this defeat, the Texans won independence after the Battle of San Jacinto, where Sam Houston led his army to a quick and decisive victory. This success created the Republic of Texas, which would later become part of the United States.

---

4. How a Bill Becomes a Law

A bill starts with an idea for a new law. A member of Congress writes the bill and introduces it. The bill is then sent to a committee where it is reviewed and debated. If the committee approves the bill, it goes to the House of Representatives and the Senate for a vote. If both pass the bill, it is sent to the president. The president can sign the bill into law or veto it. If vetoed, Congress can override the veto with a two-thirds vote. This process ensures laws are carefully examined before becoming official.

---

5. The Economic Impacts of Artificial Intelligence

Artificial intelligence, or AI, is transforming the way people work and how businesses operate. AI-powered technologies, like robots and smart software, can complete tasks faster and with fewer errors than humans. This helps companies save money and increase productivity. However, some jobs, such as assembly line work, are being replaced by AI, which raises concerns about job loss. On the other hand, AI creates new opportunities in fields like technology development and data analysis. As AI continues to grow, businesses and governments must address its challenges while ensuring its benefits are shared by all.

These passages are ideal for fluency practice and can help students strengthen their reading skills while engaging with meaningful social studies content. Use them in timed readings, group activities, or independent practice!

APPENDIX B

Metacognition Resources

Think About Your Thinking

Read the following passages with pause points. At the pause point pose the question stated to your students. Read the script, or reword into your own words, the thinking that could be happening based on the paragraph that was just completed. It is especially effective when you show your thinking out loud by using a unique voice to engage your students. The purpose of this activity is to teach them that as we read we should also be thinking about what we are reading.

The following passages are based on the content areas of science, social studies, technology, health, physical education, music, and fine arts.

The Importance of Being a Good Citizen

Being a good citizen is essential for the well-being of your community and the strength of your country. At the local level, good citizenship means taking an active role in improving your neighborhood. Simple actions like helping a neighbor, picking up litter, or attending community events make a big difference. When you support your local area, you create a stronger, more vibrant community for everyone.

[Thought to Think About: "How can I make my neighborhood a better place?"]
"Pause here and think about this: What have you done recently to improve your community? Did you help a neighbor or clean up a park? Even small actions can inspire others to contribute. Let's take a moment to imagine what a community full of helpful neighbors would look like."

At the state level, being a good citizen involves staying informed about local laws, policies, and elections. Voting in state elections helps choose leaders and policies that reflect what's important to you. When citizens actively participate, the state grows stronger and more aligned with the needs of its people.

[Thought to Think About: "Why is it important for me to participate in state elections?"]
"Let's pause for a moment to consider this: What happens if people don't vote? Who would decide the laws or leaders for your state? Think about how your voice can make a difference when you participate."

On a national level, good citizens show respect for others, regardless of differences, and work toward fairness and justice. By advocating for positive change and upholding the values of kindness and inclusion, you help build a stronger, united country.

[Thought to Think About: "What can I do to make my country better for everyone?"]
"Take a moment to reflect on this: How does treating others with respect and fairness make the country stronger? Imagine the power of millions of people working together for a common good."

Good citizenship begins with you—your actions, choices, and willingness to contribute.

The Importance of Being a Good Citizen

Being a good citizen is essential for the well-being of your community and the strength of your country. At the local level, good citizenship means taking an active role in improving your neighborhood. Simple actions like helping a neighbor, picking up litter, or attending community events make a big difference. When you support your local area, you create a stronger, more vibrant community for everyone.

At the state level, being a good citizen involves staying informed about local laws, policies, and elections. Voting in state elections helps choose leaders and policies that reflect what's important to you. When citizens actively participate, the state grows stronger and more aligned with the needs of its people.

On a national level, good citizens show respect for others, regardless of differences, and work toward fairness and justice. By advocating for positive change and upholding the values of kindness and inclusion, you help build a stronger, united country.

Good citizenship begins with you—your actions, choices, and willingness to contribute.

The Importance of the Texas Declaration of Independence

The Texas Declaration of Independence, signed on March 2, 1836, marked a pivotal moment in history, as it declared Texas's separation from Mexico. Modeled after the U.S. Declaration of Independence, this document listed grievances against the Mexican government, such as the denial of rights, lack of representation, and refusal to provide trial by jury. The declaration signified a bold step toward self-governance and freedom for Texas settlers.

[Thought to Think About: "What would it feel like to live without basic rights?"]
"Pause for a moment and imagine this: What if you were told you couldn't have a say in the laws that affect your life or that you couldn't speak freely about what you believe? Think about how the settlers must have felt and why they believed declaring independence was their only choice."

The document was signed at Washington-on-the-Brazos by 59 delegates who represented the people of Texas. These individuals risked everything—land, safety, and even their lives—because they believed freedom was worth the cost. The declaration united the settlers and set the foundation for the Republic of Texas, a new nation built on the ideals of liberty and justice.

[Thought to Think About: "What does it take to stand up for something you believe in?"]
"Take a moment to reflect: Would you be willing to take a risk like the Texas settlers did? Why do you think they were so determined to declare independence despite the dangers?"

The Texas Declaration of Independence remains a powerful symbol of courage and perseverance. It reminds Texans of the sacrifices made to establish their identity and the importance of protecting the freedoms they enjoy today.

[Thought to Think About: "How does this history shape Texas today?"]
"Now, think about this: How might Texas be different if the settlers hadn't declared independence? How does knowing this history help us appreciate the state we live in?"

The Importance of the Texas Declaration of Independence

The Texas Declaration of Independence, signed on March 2, 1836, marked a pivotal moment in history, as it declared Texas's separation from Mexico. Modeled after the U.S. Declaration of Independence, this document listed grievances against the Mexican government, such as the denial of rights, lack of representation, and refusal to provide trial by jury. The declaration signified a bold step toward self-governance and freedom for Texas settlers.

The document was signed at Washington-on-the-Brazos by 59 delegates who represented the people of Texas. These individuals risked everything—land, safety, and even their lives—because they believed freedom was worth the cost. The declaration united the settlers and set the foundation for the Republic of Texas, a new nation built on the ideals of liberty and justice.

The Texas Declaration of Independence remains a powerful symbol of courage and perseverance. It reminds Texans of the sacrifices made to establish their identity and the importance of protecting the freedoms they enjoy today.

The Importance of Long- and Short-Term Goals

Setting both long-term and short-term goals is essential for achieving success in life. Long-term goals provide direction and a sense of purpose. They are the "big picture" dreams, like earning a college degree, starting a business, or running a marathon. Short-term goals, on the other hand, are the smaller steps that lead to these achievements. These might include completing a homework assignment, saving a specific amount of money, or running a mile every day.

[Thought to Think About: "Why are small steps important to reach big dreams?"]
"Pause for a moment and imagine climbing a mountain. Would you try to leap to the top in one jump, or would you take it one step at a time? Think about how short-term goals are like those small steps, each one bringing you closer to the summit."

One of the most important aspects of goal-setting is planning. Breaking down a long-term goal into manageable, short-term tasks makes even the largest objectives feel achievable. This not only reduces stress but also helps you track progress and stay motivated.

[Thought to Think About: "How do goals keep you motivated?"]
"Think about a time when you accomplished something important. How did it feel to check off smaller tasks along the way? Consider how setting goals can keep you focused and give you a sense of accomplishment."

Both types of goals work together to build skills like time management, resilience, and focus. While short-term goals provide quick wins that boost confidence, long-term goals help you stay committed to your bigger vision.

[Thought to Think About: "What's a long-term goal you have, and what short-term steps can help you get there?"]
"Take a moment to picture one of your dreams. Now, ask yourself: What's one small step you could take today to move closer to that goal?"

The Importance of Long- and Short-Term Goals

Setting both long-term and short-term goals is essential for achieving success in life. Long-term goals provide direction and a sense of purpose. They are the "big picture" dreams, like earning a college degree, starting a business, or running a marathon. Short-term goals, on the other hand, are the smaller steps that lead to these achievements. These might include completing a homework assignment, saving a specific amount of money, or running a mile every day.

One of the most important aspects of goal-setting is planning. Breaking down a long-term goal into manageable, short-term tasks makes even the largest objectives feel achievable. This not only reduces stress but also helps you track progress and stay motivated.

Both types of goals work together to build skills like time management, resilience, and focus. While short-term goals provide quick wins that boost confidence, long-term goals help you stay committed to your bigger vision.

The Importance of Resolving Conflict and Handling Winning and Losing

Conflict is a natural part of life. Whether it's a disagreement with a friend, a sibling, or a classmate, knowing how to resolve conflict in a socially acceptable way is a skill that everyone needs. Good communication is key. Listening to the other person's perspective, calmly expressing your own feelings, and working together to find a solution are steps that can turn a disagreement into an opportunity for growth.

[Thought to Think About: "How can listening help resolve a conflict?"]
"Pause and think about a time you felt frustrated because no one listened to you. How did that make you feel? Now imagine being the person who listens—how could that change the outcome of a conflict?"

Conflict resolution also teaches us to handle winning and losing gracefully. When we win, it's important to celebrate without bragging or making others feel bad. A great response might be, "That was a fun game! You played really well." When we lose, it's okay to feel disappointed, but it's important to respond with kindness and respect, such as saying, "Good job! You deserved that win."

[Thought to Think About: "What's a positive way to respond to winning or losing?"]
"Imagine you just lost a game to a friend. How could your words show that you care about your friendship more than the outcome of the game?"

By resolving conflict respectfully and handling winning and losing with grace, we build stronger relationships. These skills help us show empathy, manage emotions, and grow as individuals.

[Thought to Think About: "Why is it important to show respect in both conflict and competition?"]
"Take a moment to consider how respect can turn a tough situation into a positive experience. What could you do differently the next time you face a conflict or lose a game?"

The Importance of Resolving Conflict and Handling Winning and Losing

Conflict is a natural part of life. Whether it's a disagreement with a friend, a sibling, or a classmate, knowing how to resolve conflict in a socially acceptable way is a skill that everyone needs. Good communication is key. Listening to the other person's perspective, calmly expressing your own feelings, and working together to find a solution are steps that can turn a disagreement into an opportunity for growth.

Conflict resolution also teaches us to handle winning and losing gracefully. When we win, it's important to celebrate without bragging or making others feel bad. A great response might be, "That was a fun game! You played really well." When we lose, it's okay to feel disappointed, but it's important to respond with kindness and respect, such as saying, "Good job! You deserved that win."

By resolving conflict respectfully and handling winning and losing with grace, we build stronger relationships. These skills help us show empathy, manage emotions, and grow as individuals.

How Art Often Imitates Real Life

Art has always been a reflection of the world around us. From ancient cave paintings that depicted hunting scenes to modern-day photography capturing moments of social change, artists draw inspiration from real-life experiences, emotions, and events. Art allows us to see the beauty, struggles, and complexity of life from different perspectives. A painter might recreate the serene beauty of a sunset, while a poet could capture the joy of friendship or the sorrow of loss.

[Thought to Think About: "How does art reflect the world you see every day?"]
"Pause for a moment and think about a painting, song, or movie that felt like it captured something from your own life. How did it make you feel to see your experiences reflected in art?"

Beyond just reflecting life, art often helps us understand it better. For example, novels and plays can explore social issues, showing us how others think and feel. Think about how a story like *Charlotte's Web* teaches us about friendship and loss, or how songs often tell stories of love, hardship, or joy. These works not only entertain us but also invite us to reflect on our own lives.

[Thought to Think About: "Why do you think artists often choose real-life moments as their inspiration?"]
"Think about why someone might write a song about overcoming challenges or paint a picture of a busy city street. How do these creations help others connect with their own experiences?"

Art also inspires action. A photograph of a polluted river can motivate efforts to clean the environment, and a play about injustice can spark conversations about equality. By imitating real life, art becomes a powerful tool for change and connection.

[Thought to Think About: "How can art encourage people to make the world better?"]
"Imagine seeing a painting that makes you feel hopeful or a movie that inspires you to help

How Art Often Imitates Real Life

Art has always been a reflection of the world around us. From ancient cave paintings that depicted hunting scenes to modern-day photography capturing moments of social change, artists draw inspiration from real-life experiences, emotions, and events. Art allows us to see the beauty, struggles, and complexity of life from different perspectives. A painter might recreate the serene beauty of a sunset, while a poet could capture the joy of friendship or the sorrow of loss.

Beyond just reflecting life, art often helps us understand it better. For example, novels and plays can explore social issues, showing us how others think and feel. Think about how a story like *Charlotte's Web* teaches us about friendship and loss, or how songs often tell stories of love, hardship, or joy. These works not only entertain us but also invite us to reflect on our own lives.

Art also inspires action. A photograph of a polluted river can motivate efforts to clean the environment, and a play about injustice can spark conversations about equality. By imitating real life, art becomes a powerful tool for change and connection.

The Similarities and Differences
Between Formal and Informal Musical Performances

Musical performances can take place in many settings, ranging from grand concert halls to casual living rooms. While formal and informal performances share the goal of showcasing musical talent, they differ in their structure, atmosphere, and audience expectations.

Formal performances, like symphony concerts or recitals, typically follow a strict program. Musicians often wear formal attire, such as tuxedos or gowns, to reflect the event's importance. The audience is expected to remain silent during the performance, clapping only at designated times. These events highlight precision, discipline, and respect for the artistry and effort behind the music.

[Thought to Think About: "What might make a formal performance feel so special?"]
"Think about attending a symphony orchestra in a concert hall. How does the setting, such as the lighting and the seating arrangement, make it different from a casual music event?"

On the other hand, informal performances, like jam sessions or backyard concerts, are more relaxed. Musicians might improvise, experiment with their music, or invite audience participation. These settings encourage connection and creativity. The audience may feel free to react openly, whether by clapping, singing along, or even dancing.

Despite their differences, both types of performances celebrate music and bring people together. Formal events often aim to preserve tradition, while informal performances prioritize spontaneity and accessibility.

[Thought to Think About: "Why might someone enjoy an informal performance more than a formal one—or vice versa?"]
"Picture a friend strumming a guitar at a campfire compared to a pianist performing on stage. How do these experiences make the music feel different to you?"

Ultimately, both formal and informal performances enrich our lives, offering unique ways to experience and appreciate the universal language of music.

[Thought to Think About: "How can attending different types of performances help you understand music better?"]
"Imagine trying both kinds of events—formal and informal. How might each one teach you something new about the power of music?"

The Similarities and Differences Between Formal and Informal Musical Performances

Musical performances can take place in many settings, ranging from grand concert halls to casual living rooms. While formal and informal performances share the goal of showcasing musical talent, they differ in their structure, atmosphere, and audience expectations.

Formal performances, like symphony concerts or recitals, typically follow a strict program. Musicians often wear formal attire, such as tuxedos or gowns, to reflect the event's importance. The audience is expected to remain silent during the performance, clapping only at designated times. These events highlight precision, discipline, and respect for the artistry and effort behind the music.

On the other hand, informal performances, like jam sessions or backyard concerts, are more relaxed. Musicians might improvise, experiment with their music, or invite audience participation. These settings encourage connection and creativity. The audience may feel free to react openly, whether by clapping, singing along, or even dancing.

Despite their differences, both types of performances celebrate music and bring people together. Formal events often aim to preserve tradition, while informal performances prioritize spontaneity and accessibility.

Ultimately, both formal and informal performances enrich our lives, offering unique ways to experience and appreciate the universal language of music.

The Importance of Respecting Digital Citizenship

In today's interconnected world, digital citizenship is as important as being a good citizen in your community. Respecting digital citizenship means understanding and following the rules of the online world, such as respecting intellectual property, abiding by copyrights, and practicing good digital etiquette. These habits ensure that the internet remains a safe, productive, and fair space for everyone.

When it comes to intellectual property, it's important to give credit where it's due. For example, using someone's artwork, writing, or music without permission or proper citation is like borrowing something valuable without asking. Copyright laws exist to protect creators' rights, ensuring they receive recognition and compensation for their work.

[Thought to Think About: "Why is it important to respect someone's hard work online?"]
"Think about how much effort a musician puts into writing a song or an artist puts into a drawing. How would you feel if someone claimed your work as their own?"

Digital etiquette, or "netiquette," involves treating others online with the same respect you'd show in person. This means avoiding harmful behavior like cyberbullying, using polite language, and following the rules of online platforms. For example, leaving constructive comments instead of negative ones can build a more supportive digital community.

[Thought to Think About: "How does being respectful online create a better experience for everyone?"]
"Imagine posting a video or artwork online and receiving positive, supportive feedback. How would that motivate you to share more of your talents?"

By respecting digital citizenship, you contribute to a safer, more respectful online environment. Following copyright rules and practicing good digital etiquette not only shows integrity but also helps you build a positive digital reputation, a valuable asset in today's digital age.

[Thought to Think About: "What steps can you take to be a responsible digital citizen today?"]
"Consider small changes, like giving credit for an image you use in a project or pausing before posting a comment. How might these habits show respect for others and their work?"

The Importance of Respecting Digital Citizenship

In today's interconnected world, digital citizenship is as important as being a good citizen in your community. Respecting digital citizenship means understanding and following the rules of the online world, such as respecting intellectual property, abiding by copyrights, and practicing good digital etiquette. These habits ensure that the internet remains a safe, productive, and fair space for everyone.

When it comes to intellectual property, it's important to give credit where it's due. For example, using someone's artwork, writing, or music without permission or proper citation is like borrowing something valuable without asking. Copyright laws exist to protect creators' rights, ensuring they receive recognition and compensation for their work.

Digital etiquette, or "netiquette," involves treating others online with the same respect you'd show in person. This means avoiding harmful behavior like cyberbullying, using polite language, and following the rules of online platforms. For example, leaving constructive comments instead of negative ones can build a more supportive digital community.

By respecting digital citizenship, you contribute to a safer, more respectful online environment. Following copyright rules and practicing good digital etiquette not only shows integrity but also helps you build a positive digital reputation, a valuable asset in today's digital age.

APPENDIX C

Poetry Resources

Fluency Rate

Fluency rate is the speed that you read,
Not too fast, but with just the right speed.
It's not a race to the very last page,
It's reading with purpose, no matter your age.

Too slow, and the meaning gets lost in delay,
Too fast, and the words start to blur on their way.
The goal is a rhythm that's steady and clear,
So the story or facts come alive in your ear.

Imagine a river that flows smooth and bright,
Not trickling too slowly, not rushing in fright.
That's how your reading should sound every time—
Flowing like music, a beautiful rhyme.

So practice your pacing, not too fast or too slow,
With each word and sentence, your skills will grow.
And soon you'll discover the perfect rate,
To read with fluency—and that feels great!

Fluency Accuracy

Fluency accuracy, what does it mean?
It's reading each word clear, sharp, and clean.
No skipping, no guessing, no words out of place,
Each one is important, like clues in a case.

When you read a word wrong, don't let it stay,
Pause for a moment, and fix it right away.
Accuracy matters; it helps you to know
What the story is saying, and helps your skills grow.

Like building a puzzle, each piece fits in tight,
Each word must be read so the meaning sounds right.
It's not just about going fast through the page,
It's reading with care, no matter your age.

So take your time, and focus your mind,
Read every word, the meaning you'll find.
With practice and patience, you'll soon come to see—
Fluency's strong when there's accuracy!

Fluency Prosody

Fluency prosody is all about tone,
It's how you make reading feel alive, not alone.
It's the rise and the fall, the rhythm and flow,
The way that your voice makes the story glow.

You pause for a comma, stop for a dot,
You ask with a question, "What's that? Or what?"
You shout when it's loud, you whisper when small,
Your voice helps the listener feel it all.

Prosody's music, the heart of the text,
It shows what comes now and what's coming next.
A boring flat voice makes the words seem unclear,
But with prosody, meaning is crystal and near.

So practice your phrasing, your tone, and your beat,
Make each line you read sound lively and neat.
With prosody's power, your reading will shine,
And every word spoken will truly align!

APPENDIX D

Fluency Rubric Resources

Fluency Self-Assessment Rubric

Instructions: Reflect on your reading fluency using the following criteria. Circle the description that best matches your performance for each statement, then write a short reflection on what you did well and what you can improve.

1. **Pace**
    - I read too slowly and had difficulty maintaining a steady rhythm.
    - I read slowly but tried to adjust my pace when I noticed it was too slow.
    - I read at a comfortable pace that was neither too fast nor too slow.
    - I read smoothly and confidently, with a natural rhythm.
2. **Accuracy**
    - I often misread or skipped words, and it was hard to understand the text.
    - I misread some words but tried to correct them as I went.
    - I read most words correctly and only needed a few corrections.
    - I read all the words accurately and rarely needed corrections.
3. **Expression**
    - I read with little to no expression, and my voice was flat or monotone.
    - I used some expression but didn't always match the mood or meaning of the text.
    - I read with good expression that matched the tone and mood most of the time.
    - I read with excellent expression that brought the text to life and helped convey its meaning.
4. **Phrasing**
    - I paused at the wrong places and often broke up sentences unnaturally.
    - I sometimes paused in the wrong places, but I tried to self-correct.
    - I grouped words into meaningful phrases and paused appropriately most of the time.
    - I read with smooth phrasing and paused naturally to match the text.
5. **Comprehension While Reading**
    - I struggled to focus on the meaning of the text because I was working hard on reading the words.
    - I understood parts of the text but lost track of meaning at times.
    - I understood most of the text and could explain it after reading.
    - I fully understood the text as I read and could summarize or discuss it easily.

Reflection:

- **What I did well:**
  (Write one or two sentences about your strengths.)
- **What I can improve:**
  (Write one or two sentences about areas to focus on next time.)

Goal for Next Time:
(Set a specific goal to work toward for your next reading session.)

Fluency Progress Assessment Rubric for Teachers

Instructions: Evaluate the student's reading fluency by selecting the description that best reflects their performance for each criterion. Use the notes section to document specific observations and areas for growth.

1. **Pace**
   - The student reads very slowly, with frequent hesitations that disrupt comprehension.
   - The student reads slowly but demonstrates effort to improve pacing.
   - The student reads at an appropriate, consistent pace, supporting comprehension most of the time.
   - The student reads smoothly at a natural pace that enhances comprehension.
2. **Accuracy**
   - The student struggles to decode words, frequently misreading or skipping them.
   - The student misreads some words but shows awareness and attempts to correct errors.
   - The student reads with high accuracy, making few decoding errors.
   - The student reads with excellent accuracy, rarely making errors.
3. **Expression**
   - The student reads in a monotone voice with little to no attention to punctuation or mood.
   - The student occasionally uses expression but inconsistently reflects the text's tone.
   - The student uses appropriate expression most of the time, aligning with the text's meaning and punctuation.
   - The student consistently reads with engaging expression that brings the text to life and matches its tone.
4. **Phrasing**
   - The student reads word-by-word or pauses unnaturally, disrupting the flow of sentences.
   - The student attempts to group words into phrases but pauses inappropriately at times.
   - The student reads with mostly smooth phrasing, pausing appropriately to match sentence structure.
   - The student reads fluidly, grouping words into meaningful phrases that enhance understanding.
5. **Comprehension While Reading**
   - The student struggles to focus on the meaning of the text due to difficulties with decoding or pacing.
   - The student understands parts of the text but loses meaning due to fluency challenges.
   - The student understands most of the text while reading, with minor disruptions to comprehension.
   - The student demonstrates full comprehension while reading, integrating fluency and understanding seamlessly.

Notes on Performance:
(Record specific examples of strengths and areas for growth observed during reading.)

Progress Observations:

- **Improvement Since Last Assessment:**
  (Identify areas where the student has made progress.)
- **Current Focus for Development:**
  (Suggest targeted strategies or goals to enhance fluency further.)

Overall Fluency Progress Rating:
(Choose one: Beginning, Developing, Proficient, Advanced)

APPENDIX E

Famous Quotes Resource

Here are 50 short, inspiring quotes, along with the individuals who said them, that students can memorize to improve fluency while being motivated:

Quotes for Inspiration and Fluency Practice

1. **"Believe you can and you're halfway there."** – Theodore Roosevelt
2. **"Success is not final, failure is not fatal: It is the courage to continue that counts."** – Winston Churchill
3. **"Do what you can, with what you have, where you are."** – Theodore Roosevelt
4. **"Be the change that you wish to see in the world."** – Mahatma Gandhi
5. **"It always seems impossible until it's done."** – Nelson Mandela
6. **"Strive not to be a success, but rather to be of value."** – Albert Einstein
7. **"Happiness is not something ready-made. It comes from your own actions."** – Dalai Lama
8. **"Act as if what you do makes a difference. It does."** – William James
9. **"You are never too old to set another goal or to dream a new dream."** – C.S. Lewis
10. **"Nothing is impossible. The word itself says, 'I'm possible!'"** – Audrey Hepburn

Quotes about Learning and Growth

11. **"Education is the most powerful weapon which you can use to change the world."** – Nelson Mandela
12. **"The more that you read, the more things you will know."** – Dr. Seuss
13. **"An investment in knowledge pays the best interest."** – Benjamin Franklin
14. **"Live as if you were to die tomorrow. Learn as if you were to live forever."** – Mahatma Gandhi
15. **"Wisdom begins in wonder."** – Socrates
16. **"Tell me and I forget. Teach me and I remember. Involve me and I learn."** – Benjamin Franklin
17. **"The beautiful thing about learning is that no one can take it away from you."** – B.B. King
18. **"In learning, you will teach, and in teaching, you will learn."** – Phil Collins
19. **"Once you learn to read, you will be forever free."** – Frederick Douglass
20. **"Curiosity is the wick in the candle of learning."** – William Arthur Ward

Quotes About Perseverance

21. **"Fall seven times and stand up eight."** – Japanese Proverb
22. **"Perseverance is not a long race; it is many short races one after the other."** – Walter Elliot
23. **"Our greatest glory is not in never falling, but in rising every time we fall."** – Confucius
24. **"Don't watch the clock; do what it does. Keep going."** – Sam Levenson
25. **"You just can't beat the person who never gives up."** – Babe Ruth
26. **"Dream big and dare to fail."** – Norman Vaughan
27. **"Success is stumbling from failure to failure with no loss of enthusiasm."** – Winston Churchill
28. **"The only way to achieve the impossible is to believe it is possible."** – Charles Kingsleigh (Alice in Wonderland)
29. **"It does not matter how slowly you go as long as you do not stop."** – Confucius
30. **"Hardships often prepare ordinary people for an extraordinary destiny."** – C.S. Lewis

Quotes About Character and Integrity

31. **"Integrity is doing the right thing, even when no one is watching."** – C.S. Lewis
32. **"Character is how you treat those who can do nothing for you."** – Unknown
33. **"Do the right thing because it is right."** – Immanuel Kant
34. **"Your character is your destiny."** – Heraclitus
35. **"It takes courage to grow up and become who you really are."** – E.E. Cummings
36. **"What lies behind us and what lies before us are tiny matters compared to what lies within us."** – Ralph Waldo Emerson
37. **"When you have a choice, choose kindness."** – Unknown
38. **"The best way to predict the future is to create it."** – Abraham Lincoln
39. **"No act of kindness, no matter how small, is ever wasted."** – Aesop
40. **"Goodness is the only investment that never fails."** – Henry David Thoreau

Quotes About Dreams and Aspirations

41. **"Shoot for the moon. Even if you miss, you'll land among the stars."** Norman Vincent Peale
42. **"The future belongs to those who believe in the beauty of their dreams."** – Eleanor Roosevelt
43. **"Dream big dreams; small dreams have no magic."** – Dottie Boreyko
44. **"Keep your eyes on the stars, and your feet on the ground."** – Theodore Roosevelt
45. **"Don't be pushed around by the fears in your mind. Be led by the dreams in your heart."** – Roy T. Bennett
46. **"All our dreams can come true if we have the courage to pursue them."** – Walt Disney

47. **"Success is not the key to happiness. Happiness is the key to success."** – Albert Schweitzer
48. **"You miss 100% of the shots you don't take."** – Wayne Gretzky
49. **"If you can dream it, you can do it."** – Walt Disney
50. **"Doubt kills more dreams than failure ever will."** – Suzy Kassem

These quotes are not only inspirational but also varied in tone, offering students ample opportunity to practice expression, pacing, and intonation as they commit them to memory.

APPENDIX F

Fluency Project Resources

Fluency Mastery Project: "The Art of Reading Aloud"

Students will work collaboratively and independently over several weeks to create a culminating "Fluency Showcase." The project will focus on understanding and applying fluency components: **rate, accuracy, and prosody.** By the end of the project, students will demonstrate their understanding through research, practice, and performance.

Introduction to Fluency: Building Understanding

Begin with a class discussion and mini-lessons that explore:

- **Rate:** How fast or slow you read.
- **Accuracy:** How correctly you read the words.
- **Prosody:** The expression, rhythm, and tone you use when reading.

Students will:

- Create fluency definition posters, including examples and non examples of each component.
- Watch video examples of different readers (e.g., too fast, too monotone, expressive) and discuss what makes each effective or ineffective.

Fluency Detective Work: Analyzing Texts

In small groups, students will analyze texts for fluency challenges.

Students will:

- Choose a passage (fiction, poetry, or informational) and highlight where:
    - **Rate** might affect understanding (e.g., fast-paced action vs. reflective dialogue).
    - **Accuracy** is crucial for meaning (e.g., words with multiple meanings or difficult vocabulary).

  - **Prosody** enhances the mood (e.g., exciting moments, questions, or dramatic pauses).
- Present their findings with examples of how a reader could improve each fluency skill in the passage.

Practice and Peer Feedback: Refining Fluency Skills

Students will select their own passages to practice reading aloud, focusing on **rate, accuracy, and prosody**.

Students will:

- Record themselves reading the passage.
- Use a fluency self-assessment rubric to reflect on their performance.
- Pair up with a peer to exchange feedback using a peer-assessment checklist, focusing on:
  - Was the rate appropriate for the text?
  - Were all words pronounced correctly?
  - Was expression used effectively?

Fluency Stations: Targeted Skill Development

Students will rotate through stations to complete activities designed to reinforce specific skills.

- **Rate Station:** Timed reading exercises to adjust speed for comprehension.
- **Accuracy Station:** Word games focusing on decoding tricky vocabulary or spotting misread words in a passage.
- **Prosody Station:** Practice reading with expression using scripts, poetry, or song lyrics.

Creative Application: Fluency in Action

Each student will apply their fluency skills to a creative task of their choice.

Options include:

- Writing and performing a skit with dialogue that requires different rates and expressions.
- Creating a short audiobook with sound effects to enhance prosody.
- Turning a nonfiction article into an engaging news report, adjusting rate and tone for emphasis.

Fluency Showcase: Demonstrating Mastery

The project will culminate in a "Fluency Showcase," where students demonstrate their mastery of **rate, accuracy, and prosody** through a public performance.

Students will:

- Choose a passage to perform (e.g., poem, story excerpt, speech, or monologue).
- Prepare a brief explanation of how they applied rate, accuracy, and prosody to make the reading effective.
- Perform their passage for the class, small groups, or an invited audience (e.g., parents, other teachers).

Assessment and Reflection

Students will be evaluated on:

- **Application of Skills:** Did the student demonstrate appropriate rate, accuracy, and prosody in their performance?
- **Understanding of Concepts:** Did the student explain how they used each fluency skill effectively?
- **Growth:** Did the student show improvement based on self- and peer-assessments?

After the showcase, students will write a reflection on their fluency journey:

- What was easy or difficult about improving their rate, accuracy, or prosody?
- How did these skills help them become better readers?
- How can they continue to use fluency in everyday reading and speaking?

This extensive project integrates research, practice, collaboration, and performance to ensure students deeply understand and apply the concepts of rate, accuracy, and prosody in fluency.

You said:

Remove the divider lines from above

ChatGPT said:

ChatGPT

Fluency Mastery Project: "The Art of Reading Aloud"

Students will work collaboratively and independently over several weeks to create a culminating "Fluency Showcase." The project will focus on understanding and applying fluency components: **rate, accuracy, and prosody.** By the end of the project, students will demonstrate their understanding through research, practice, and performance.

Introduction to Fluency: Building Understanding

Begin with a class discussion and mini-lessons that explore:

- **Rate:** How fast or slow you read.
- **Accuracy:** How correctly you read the words.
- **Prosody:** The expression, rhythm, and tone you use when reading.

Students will:

- Create fluency definition posters, including examples and non-examples of each component.
- Watch video examples of different readers (e.g., too fast, too monotone, expressive) and discuss what makes each effective or ineffective.

Fluency Detective Work: Analyzing Texts

In small groups, students will analyze texts for fluency challenges.

Students will:

- Choose a passage (fiction, poetry, or informational) and highlight where:
  - **Rate** might affect understanding (e.g., fast-paced action vs. reflective dialogue).
  - **Accuracy** is crucial for meaning (e.g., words with multiple meanings or difficult vocabulary).
  - **Prosody** enhances the mood (e.g., exciting moments, questions, or dramatic pauses).
- Present their findings with examples of how a reader could improve each fluency skill in the passage.

Practice and Peer Feedback: Refining Fluency Skills

Students will select their own passages to practice reading aloud, focusing on **rate, accuracy, and prosody**.

Students will:

- Record themselves reading the passage.
- Use a fluency self-assessment rubric to reflect on their performance.
- Pair up with a peer to exchange feedback using a peer-assessment checklist, focusing on:
  - Was the rate appropriate for the text?
  - Were all words pronounced correctly?
  - Was expression used effectively?

Fluency Stations: Targeted Skill Development

Students will rotate through stations to complete activities designed to reinforce specific skills.

- **Rate Station:** Timed reading exercises to adjust speed for comprehension.
- **Accuracy Station:** Word games focusing on decoding tricky vocabulary or spotting misread words in a passage.
- **Prosody Station:** Practice reading with expression using scripts, poetry, or song lyrics.

Creative Application: Fluency in Action

Each student will apply their fluency skills to a creative task of their choice.

Options include:

- Writing and performing a skit with dialogue that requires different rates and expressions.
- Creating a short audiobook with sound effects to enhance prosody.
- Turning a nonfiction article into an engaging news report, adjusting rate and tone for emphasis.

Fluency Showcase: Demonstrating Mastery

The project will culminate in a "Fluency Showcase," where students demonstrate their mastery of **rate, accuracy, and prosody** through a public performance.

Students will:

- Choose a passage to perform (e.g., poem, story excerpt, speech, or monologue).
- Prepare a brief explanation of how they applied rate, accuracy, and prosody to make the reading effective.
- Perform their passage for the class, small groups, or an invited audience (e.g., parents, other teachers).

Assessment and Reflection

Students will be evaluated on:

- **Application of Skills:** Did the student demonstrate appropriate rate, accuracy, and prosody in their performance?
- **Understanding of Concepts:** Did the student explain how they used each fluency skill effectively?
- **Growth:** Did the student show improvement based on self- and peer-assessments?

After the showcase, students will write a reflection on their fluency journey:

- What was easy or difficult about improving their rate, accuracy, or prosody?
- How did these skills help them become better readers?
- How can they continue to use fluency in everyday reading and speaking?

This extensive project integrates research, practice, collaboration, and performance to ensure students deeply understand and apply the concepts of rate, accuracy, and prosody in fluency.

Made in the USA
Monee, IL
01 August 2025